COLOR
Pre-Columbian Art

Conceived, Designed, and Illustrated by:

Mrinal Mitra

Series Edited by:

Swarna Mitra & **Malika Mitra**

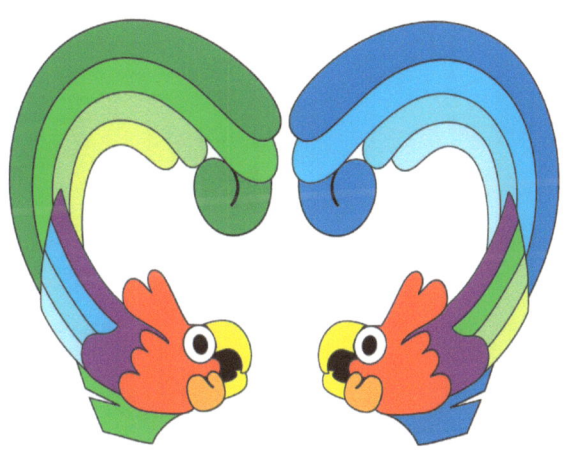

WORLD CULTURE COLORING SERIES

This series is dedicated to the citizens of the world;
from the young blooming minds of children, to the aspired individuals of all ages.

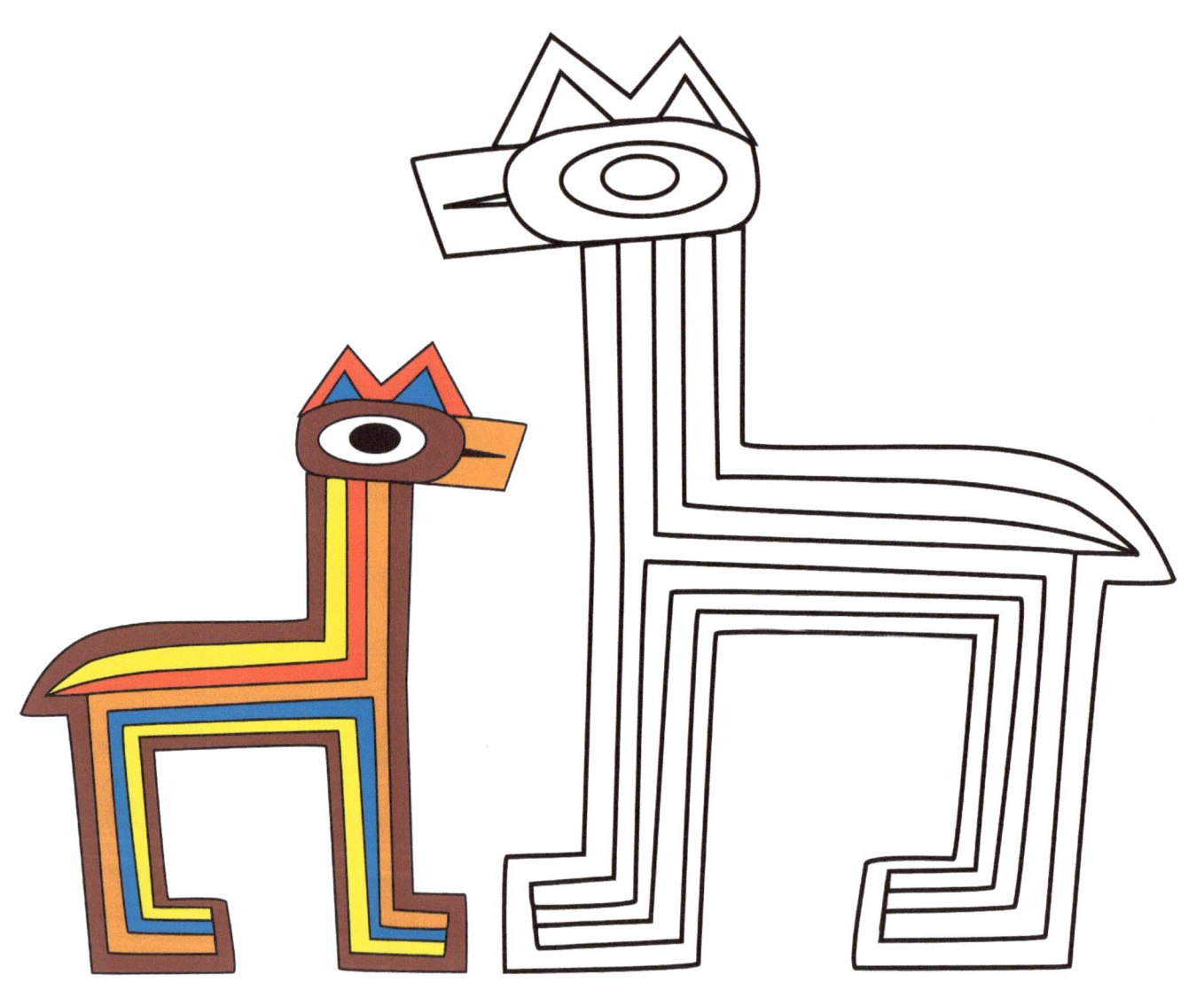

*Incas created superb patterns such as
this highly abstract shape of a llama, Saksaywaman, Peru.*

Pre-Columbian Art

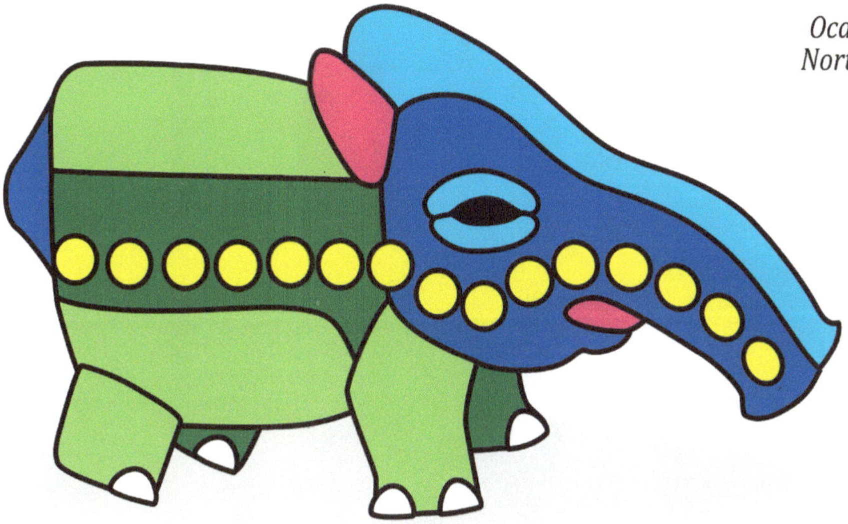

Ocarina in the form of a tapir.
Northern Guatemala highlands.

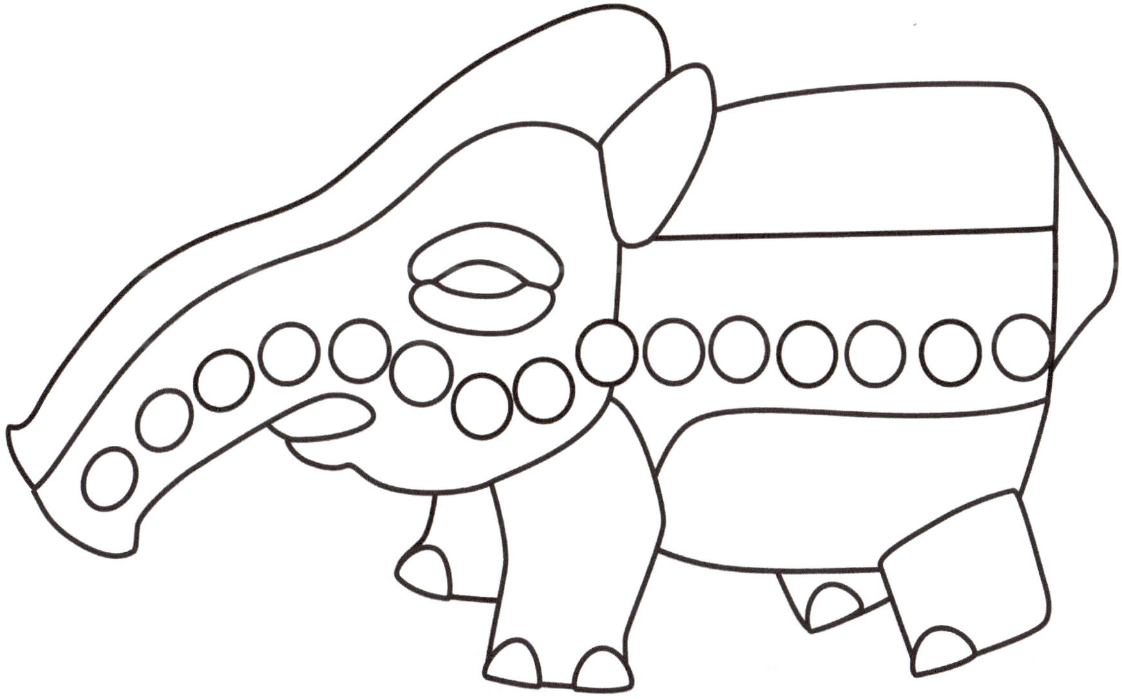

Color the drawings above using your preferred choice of colors.

3

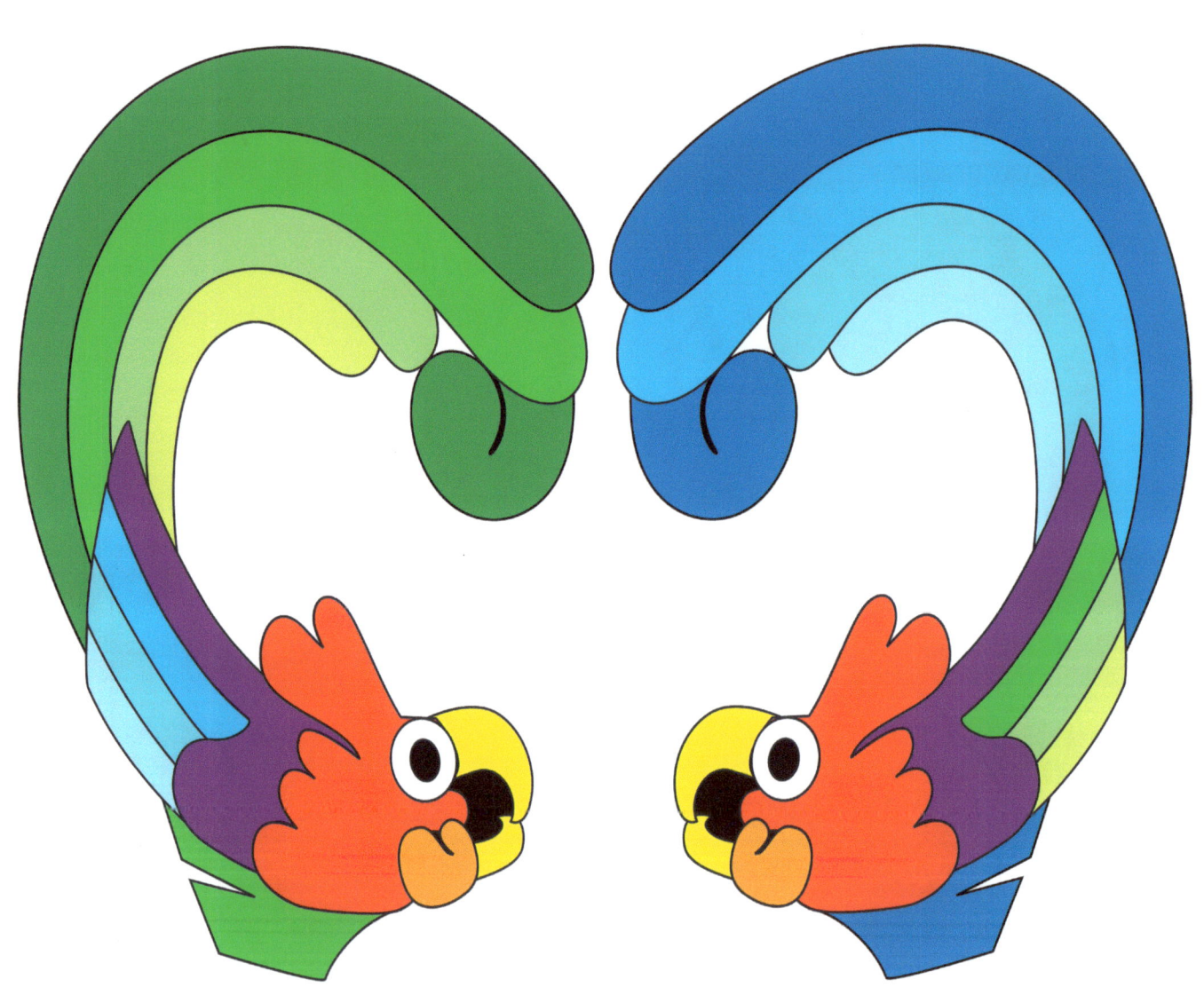

'Great Sun' or Quetzal Macaw, Mayan Civilization.

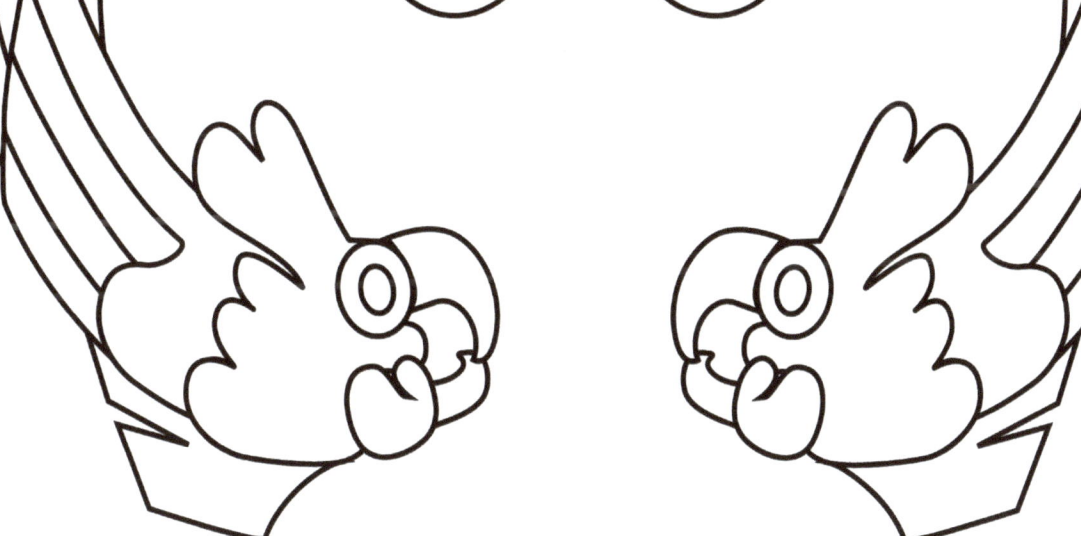

Color the drawings above using your preferred choice of colors.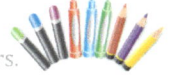

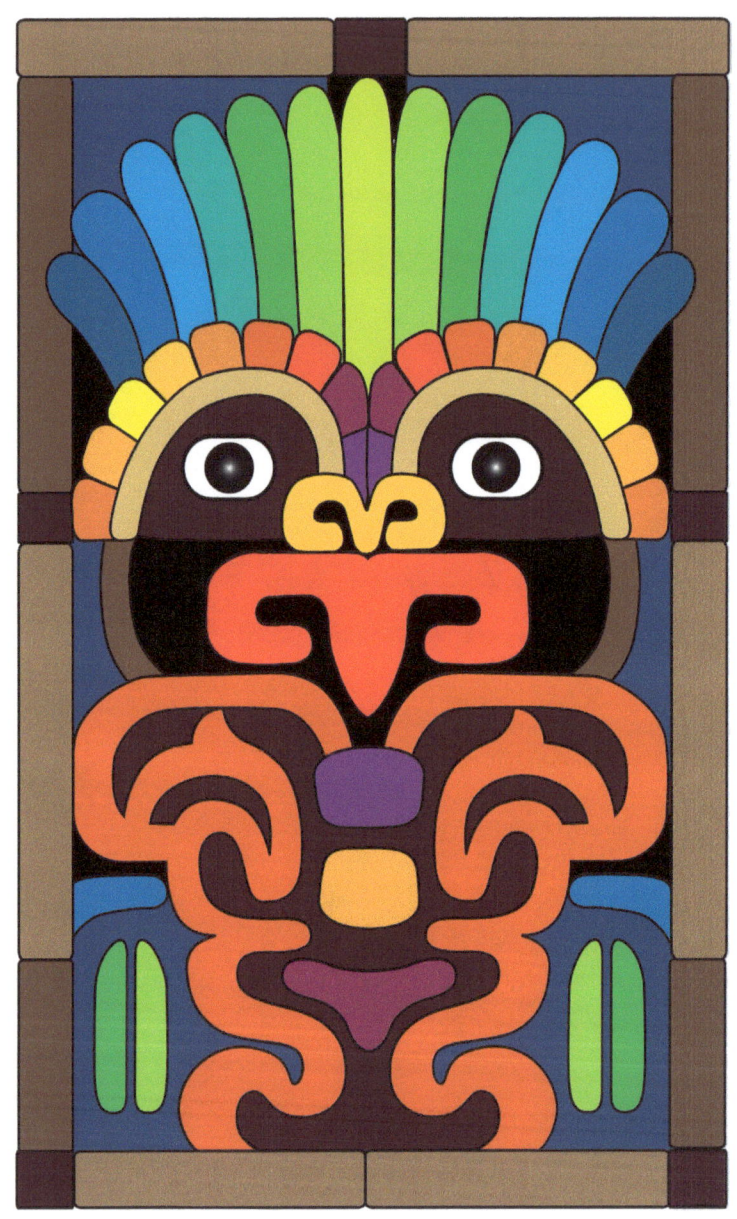

Bizarre imagery of the hybrid god, both bird and butterfly.
Uxmal, Mexico. 800 - 900 C.E.

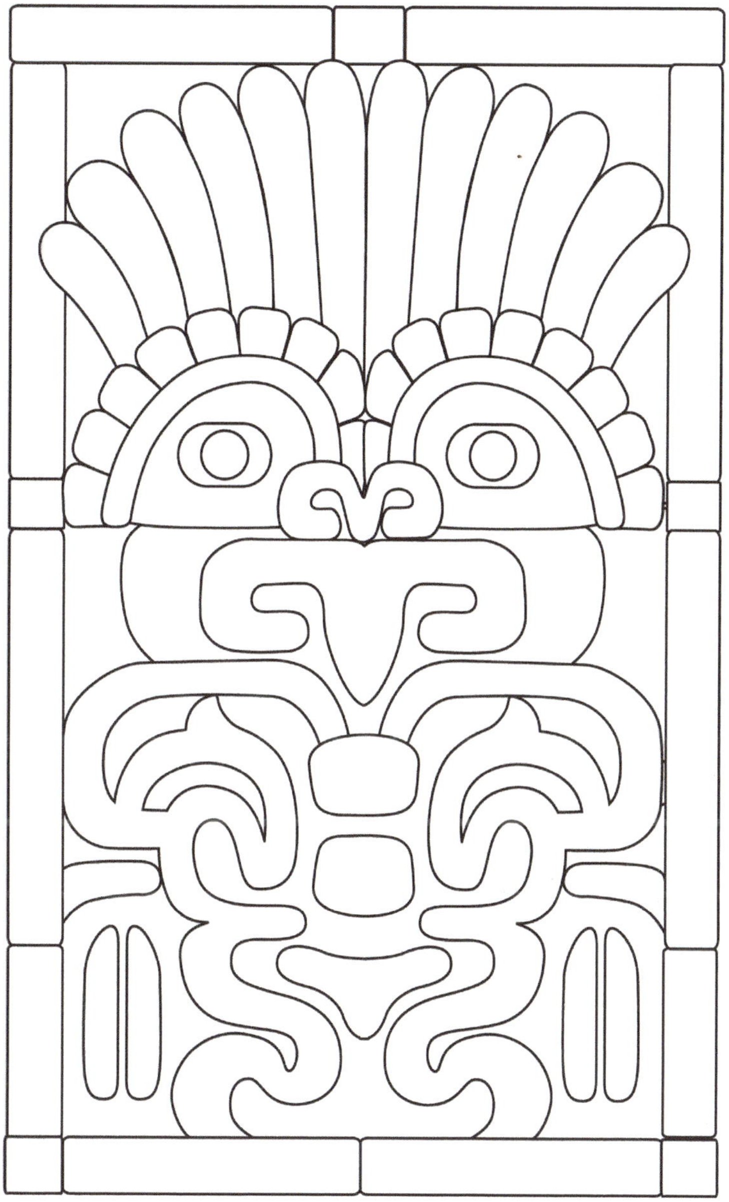

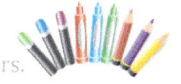

Color the drawing above using your preferred choice of colors.

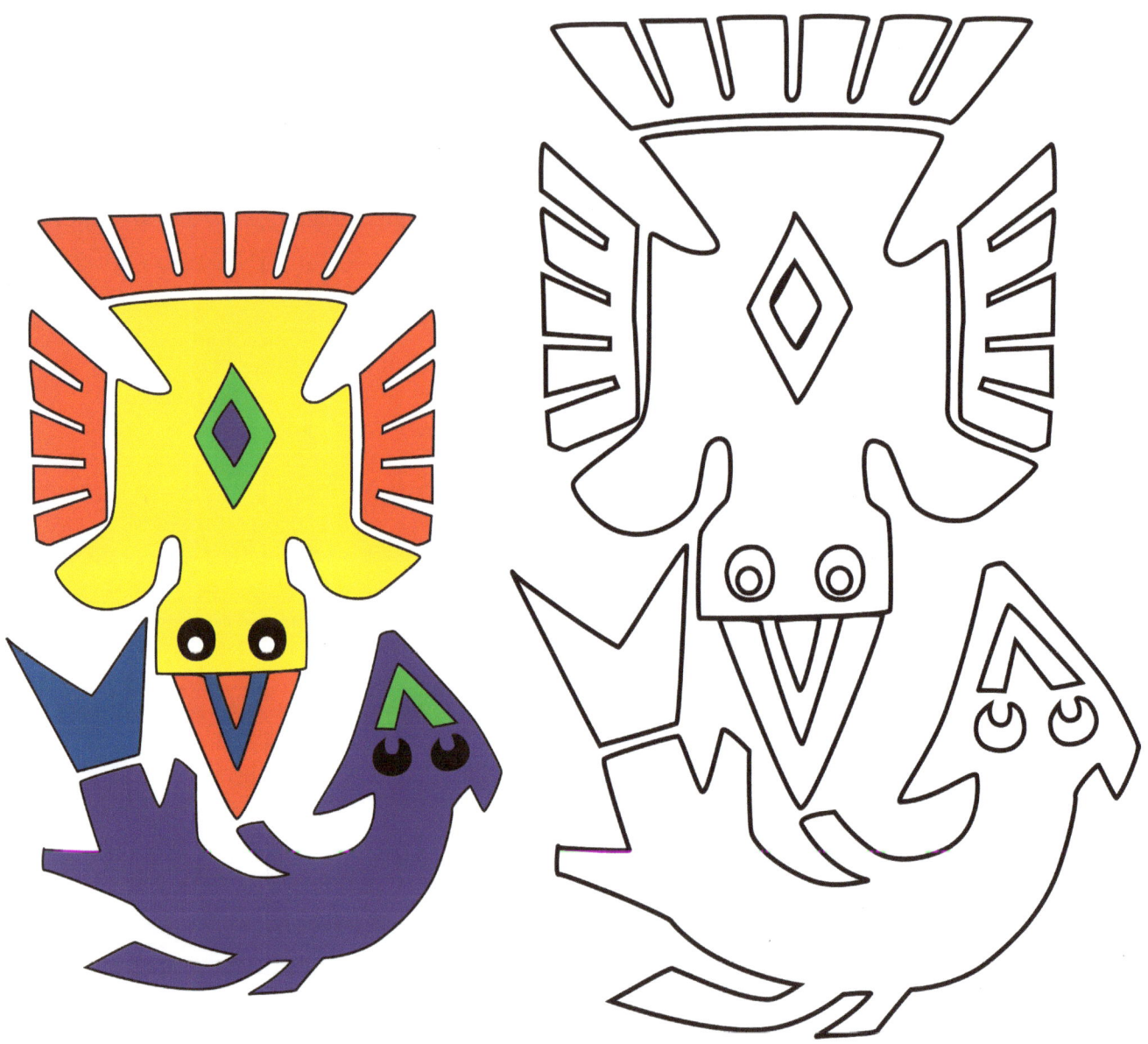

Shrouds found in Paracas, South America, are over 2000 years old and are still vivid in colors. Human figures, deities, mythological animals such as Jaguar, Serpent-Dragon, and others are depicted on a plain or checkered background.

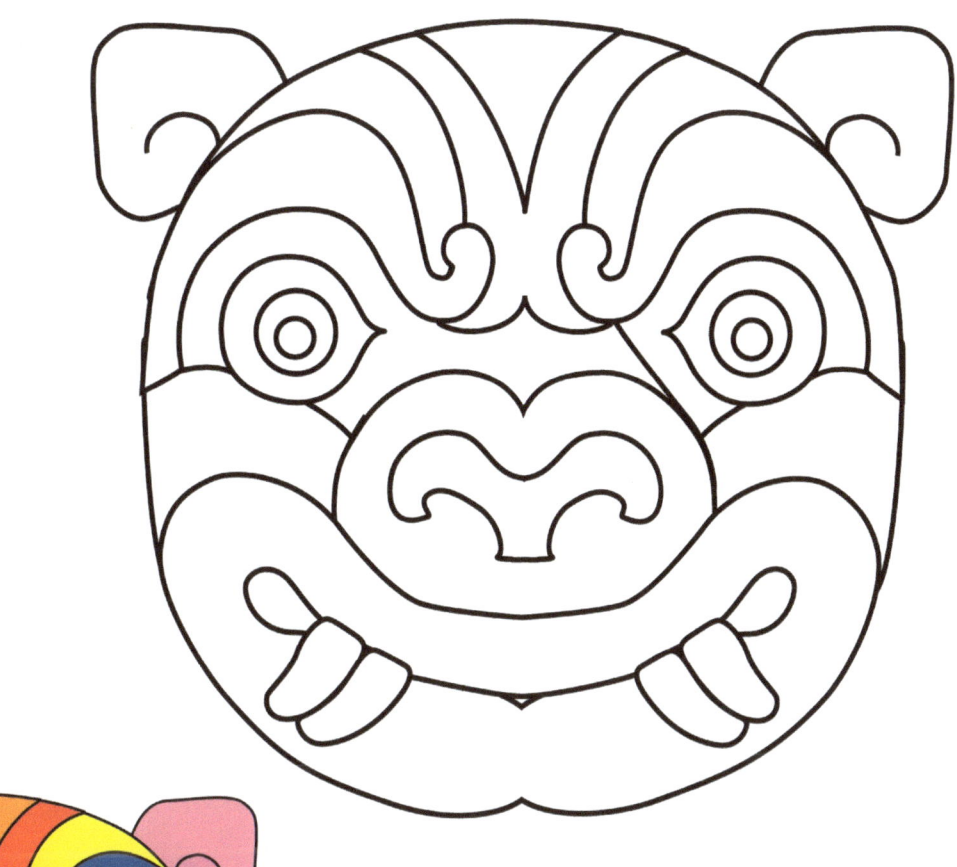

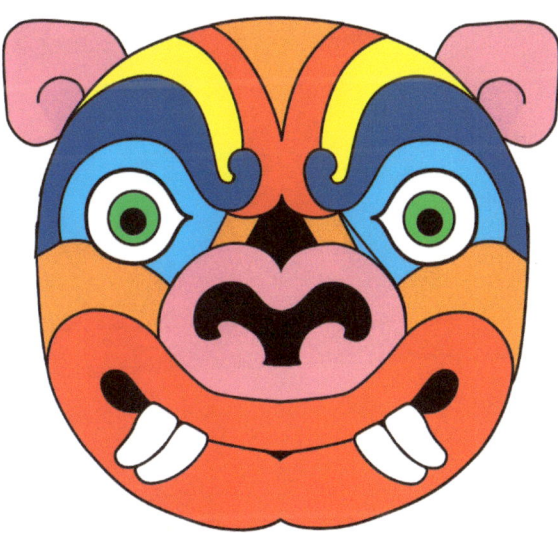

Were-Jaguar tenoned into the wall of the pyramid of Chavin. It is the earliest stone temple found in Peru (Olmec mythology).

Color the drawings above using your preferred choice of colors.

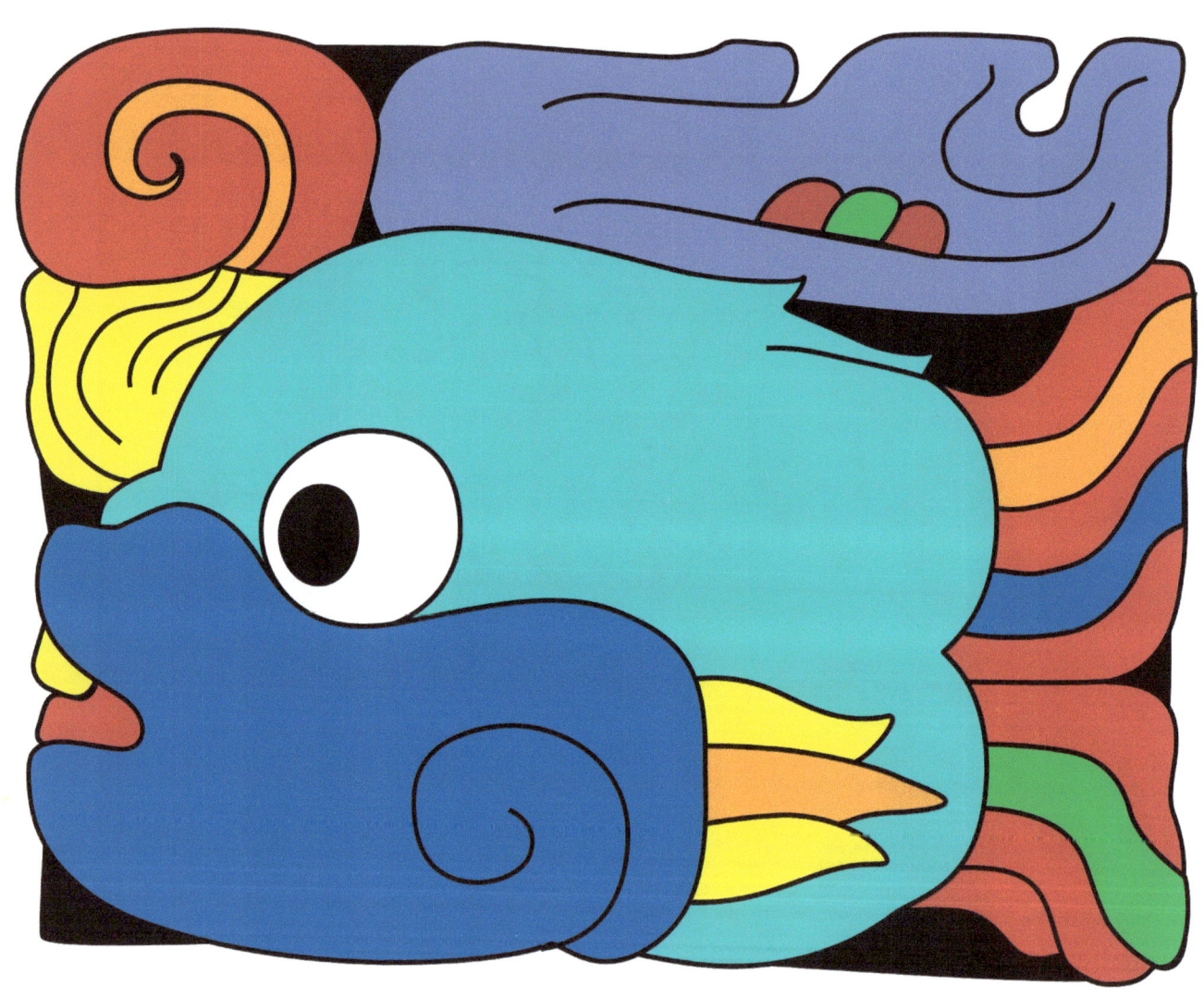

Mayan Hieroglyph
A large hieroglyph representing place and name, from Structure 10L - 22A (The Mat House). Copan civilization.

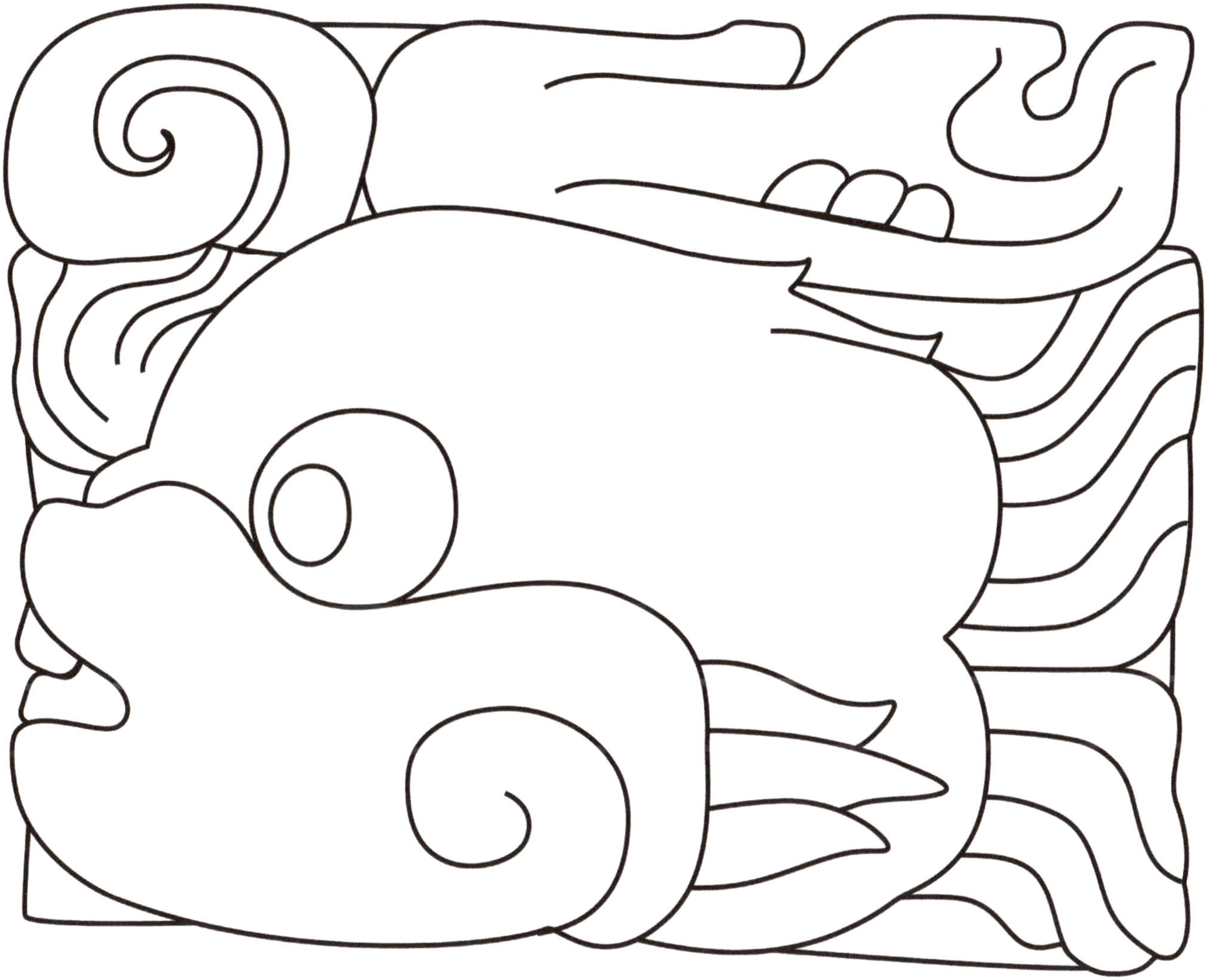

Color the drawing above using your preferred choice of colors.

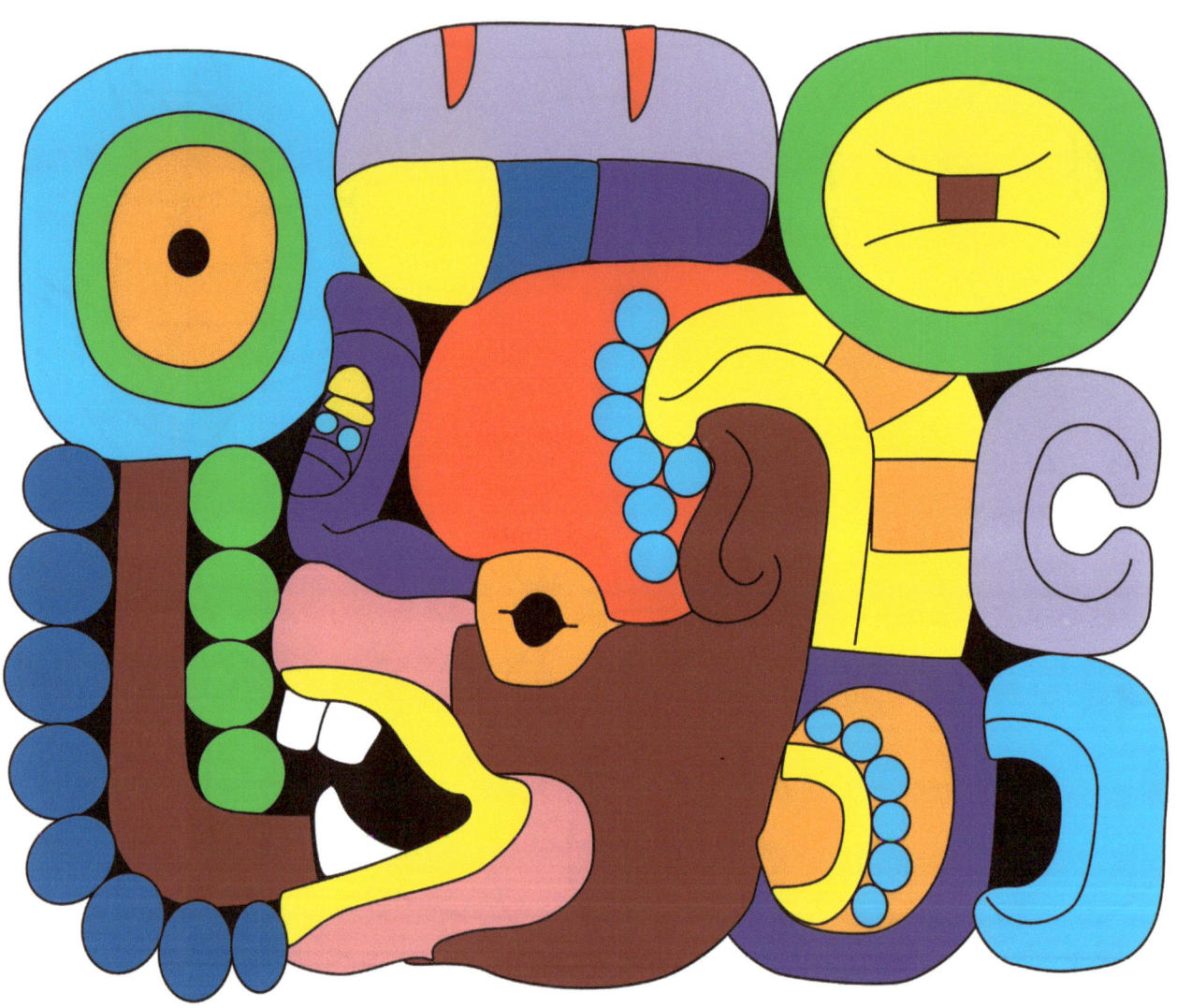

Mayan Hieroglyph

The Copan emblem-glyph. The beads on the left represent sacred drops. Two signs on the top signify the person as the Holy Lord of the kingdom. The kingdom is named by the sign of a leaf-nosed bat as shown.

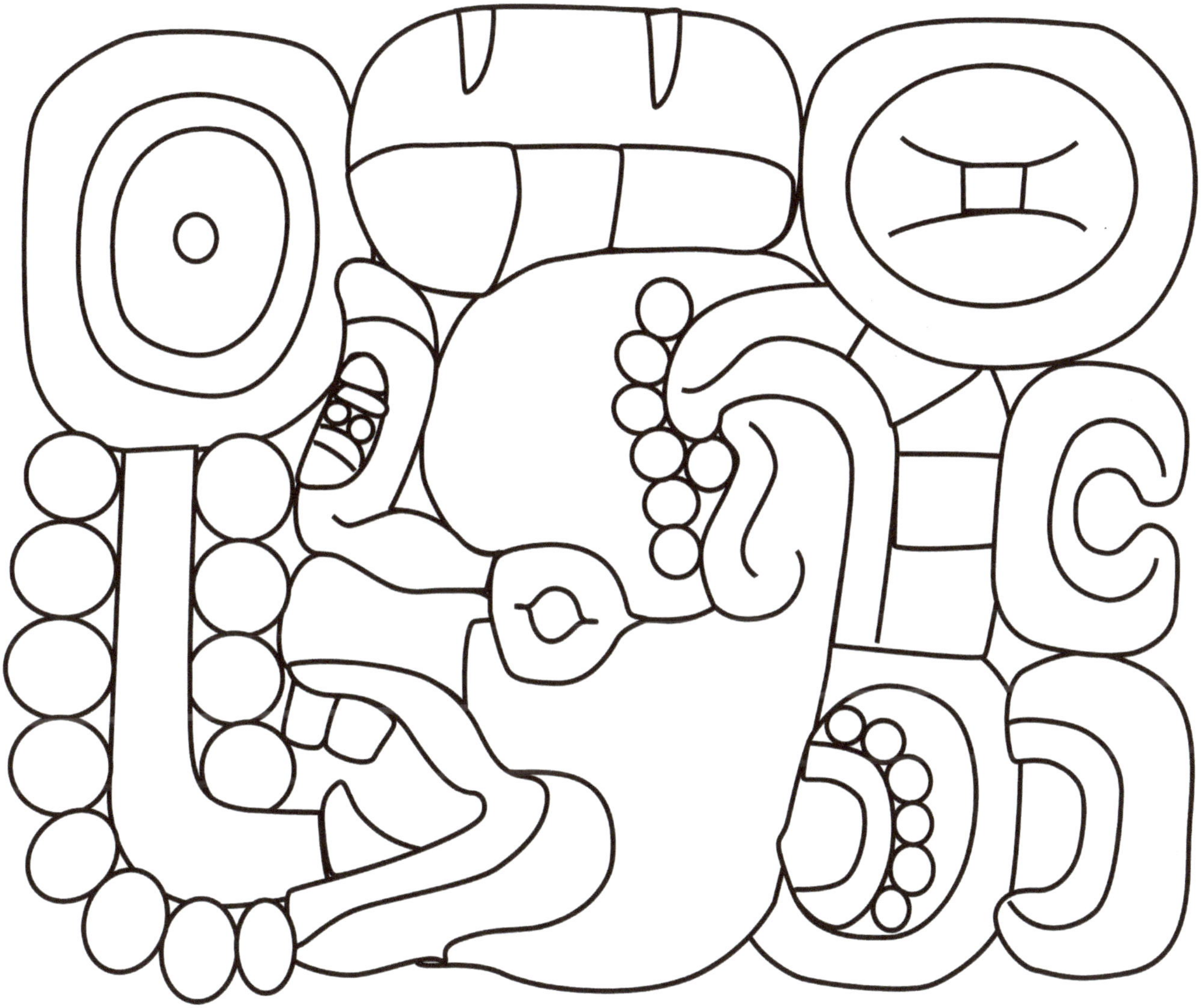

Color the drawing above using your preferred choice of colors.

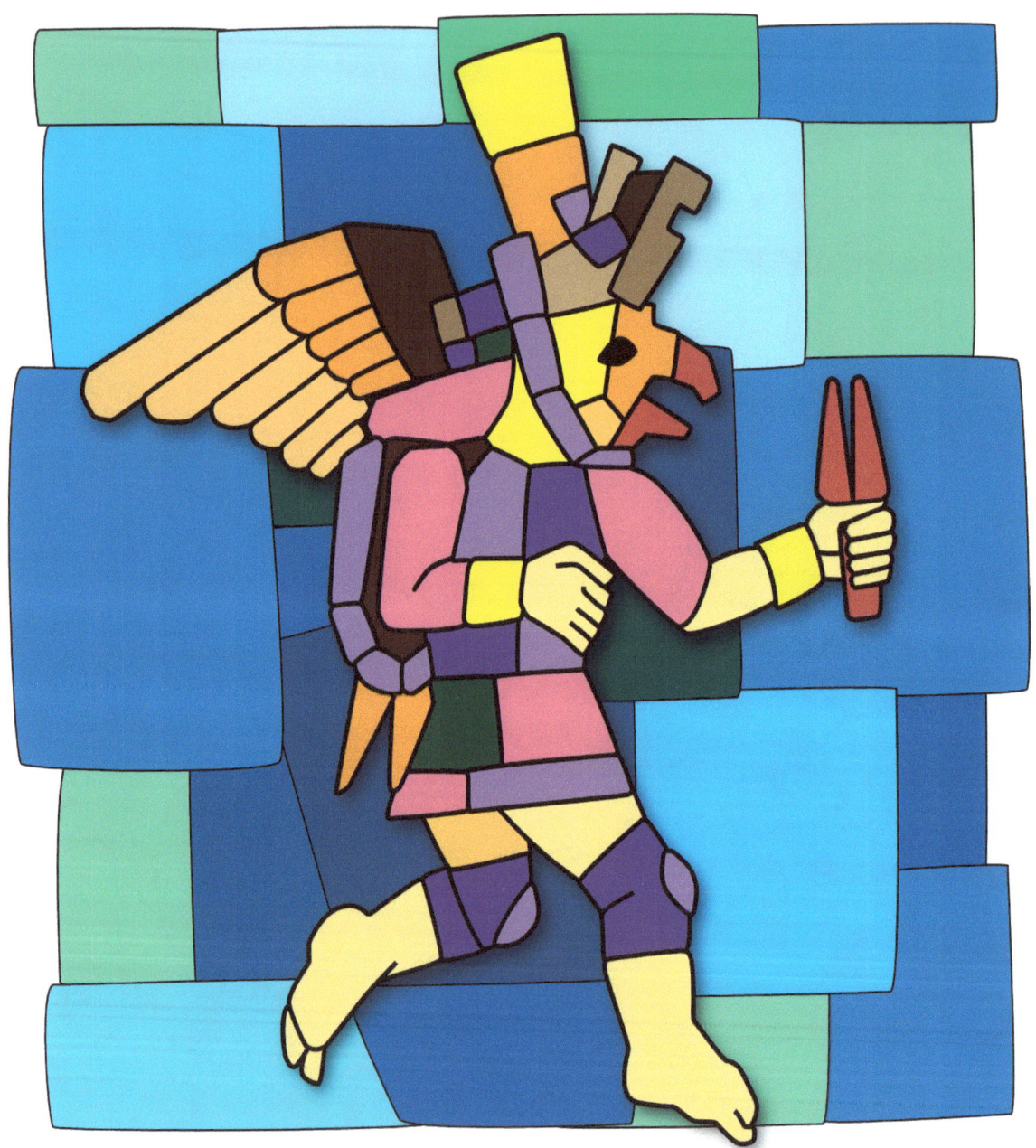

Found on a pair of Moche earplugs with bean runners.
Mochica Civilization, 100 C.E. to 800 C.E. Gold with turquoise and shell inlay.

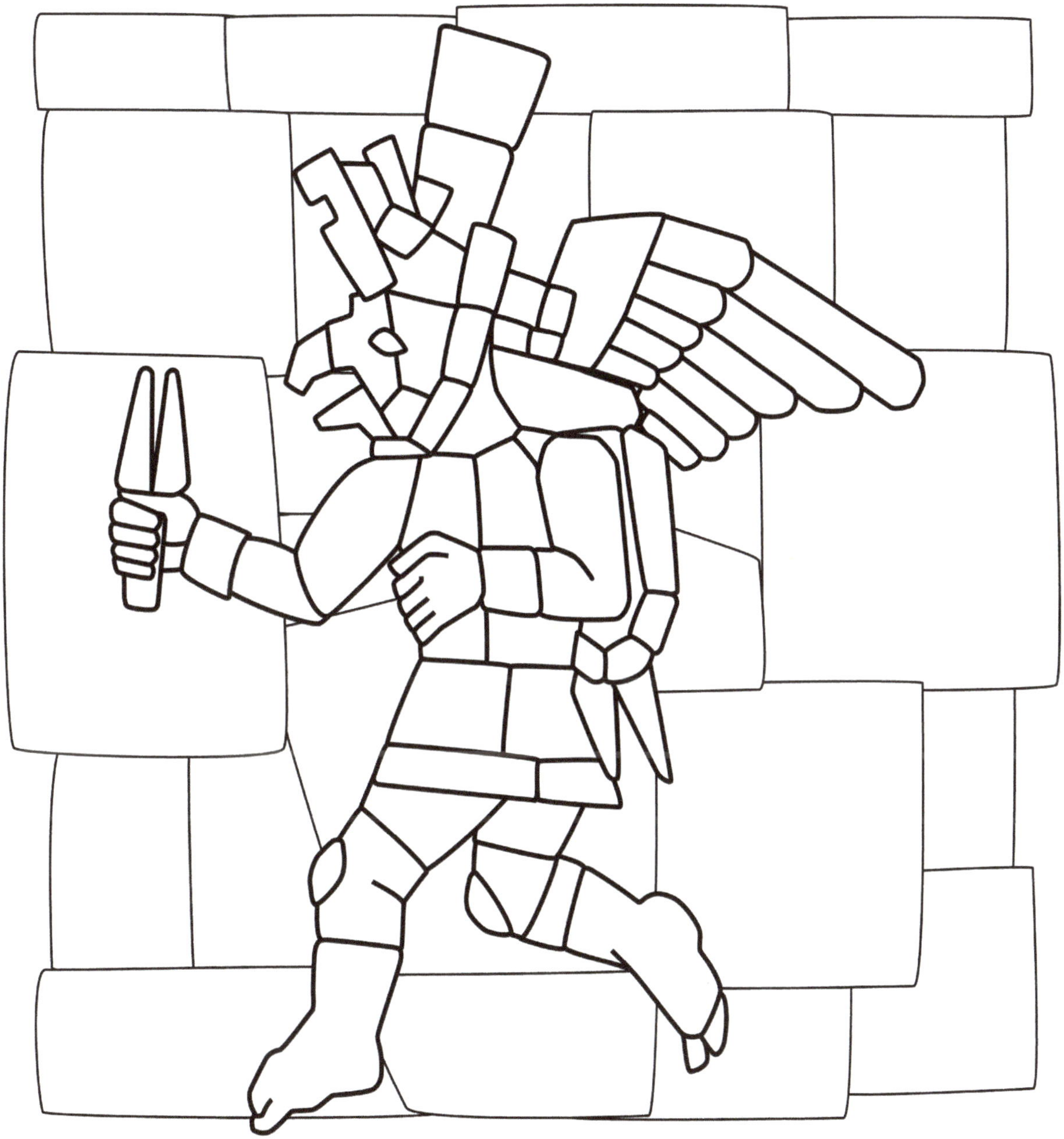

Color the drawing above using your preferred choice of colors.

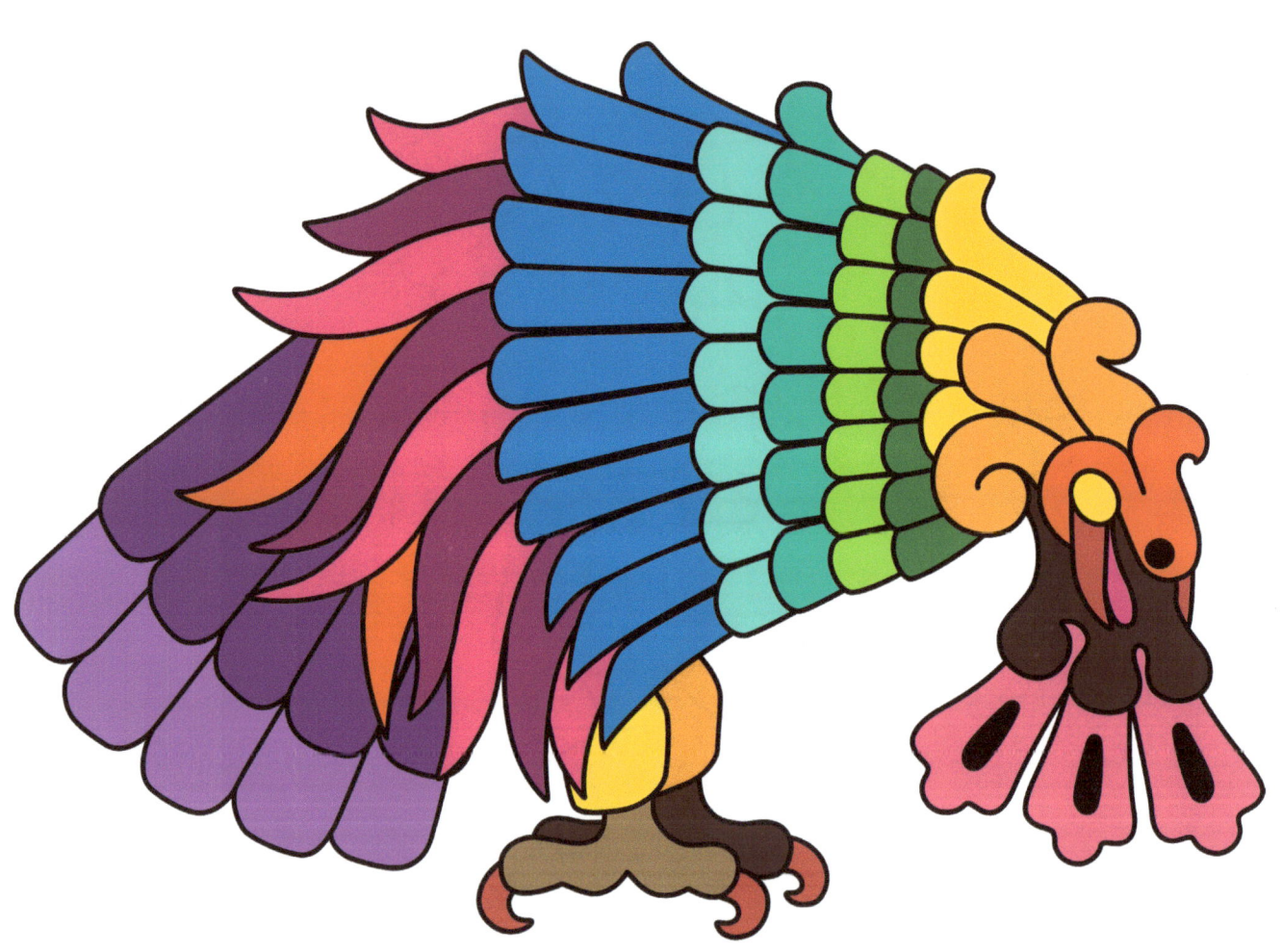

Eagle on a frieze in the temple of Quetzalcoatl, Tula.

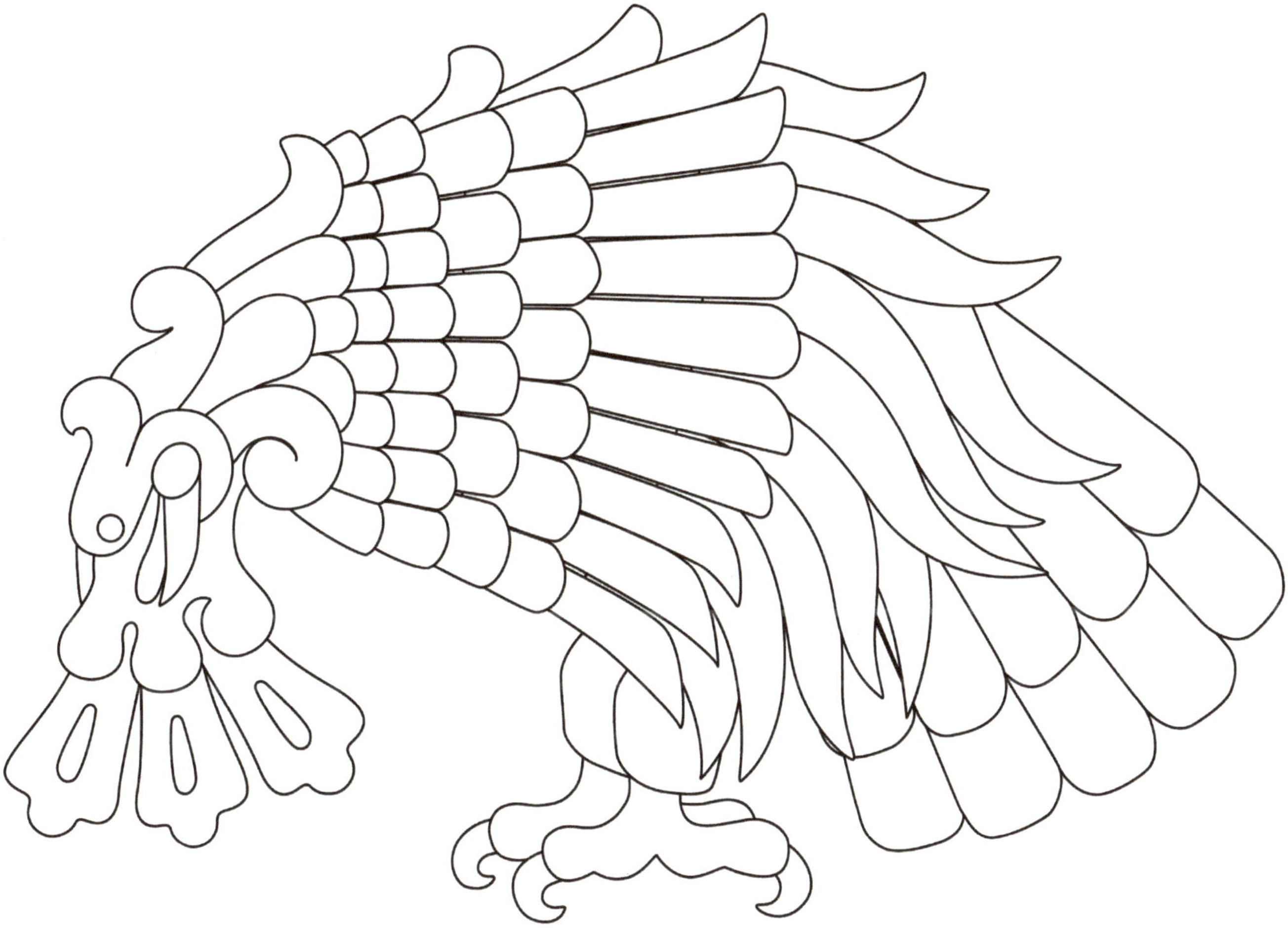

Color the drawing above using your preferred choice of colors.

17

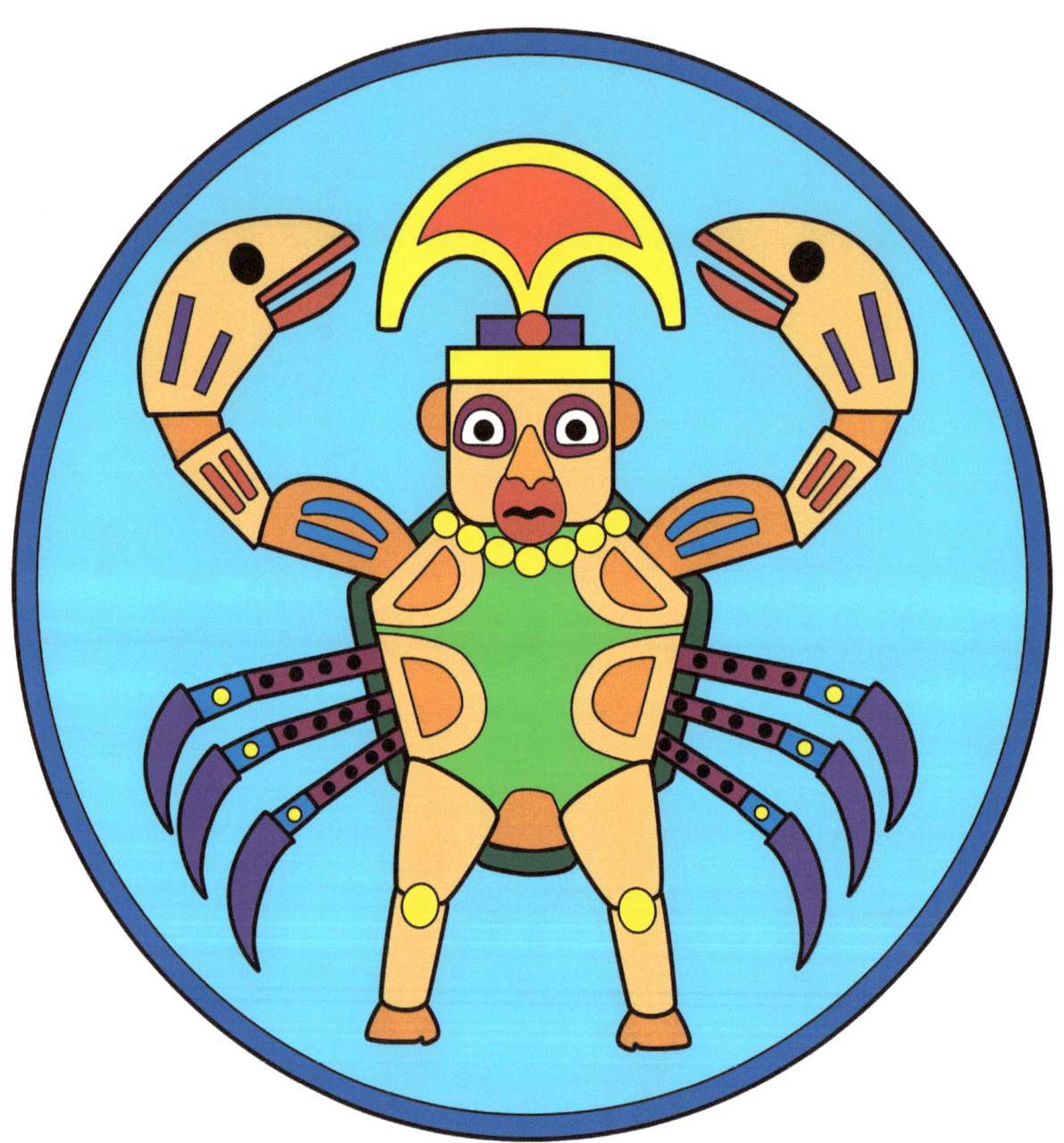

Crab God, Inca Civilization, Peru.

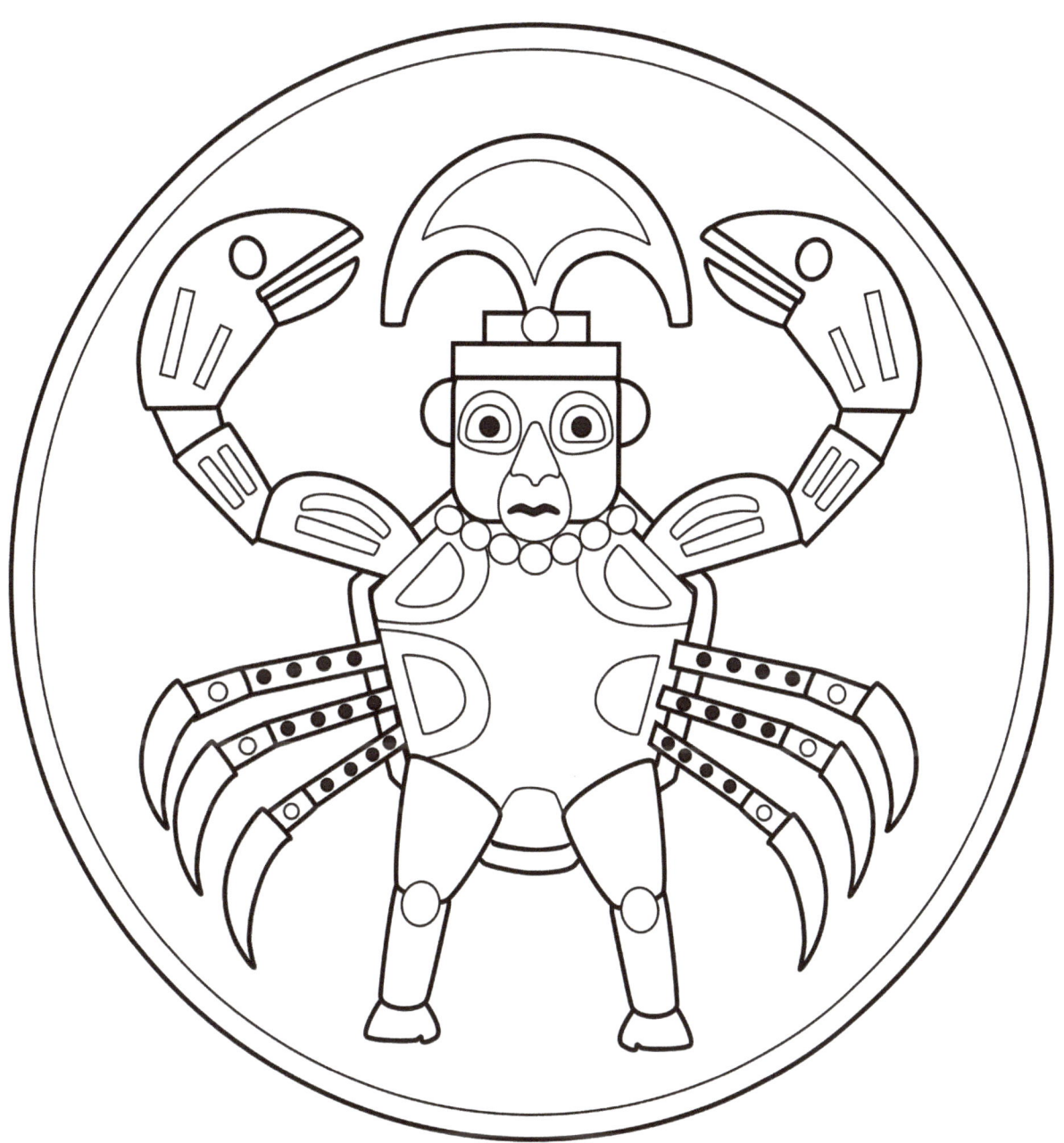

Color the drawing above using your preferred choice of colors.

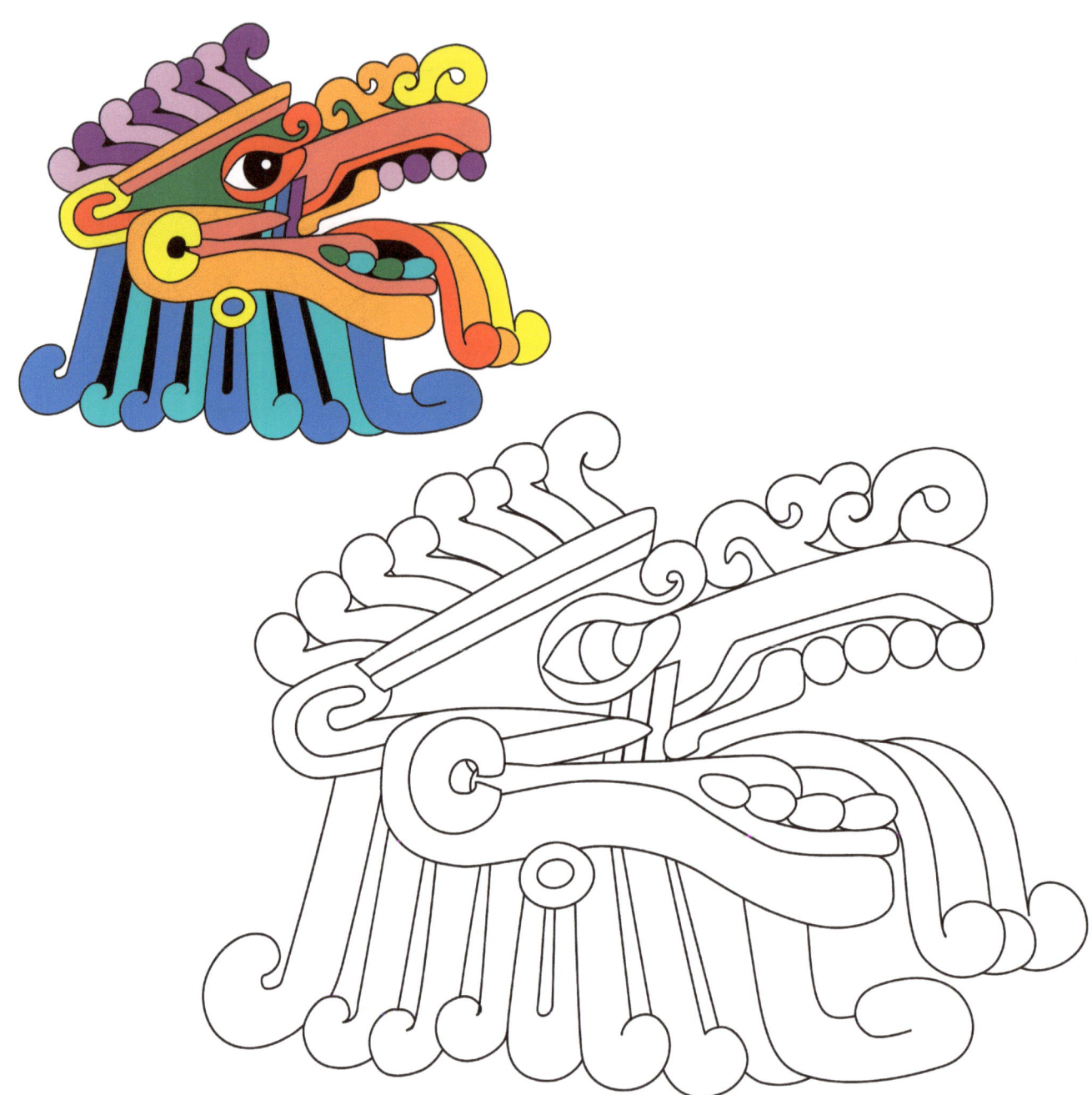

Open fanged head of a feathered serpent worshiped at Xochicalco.

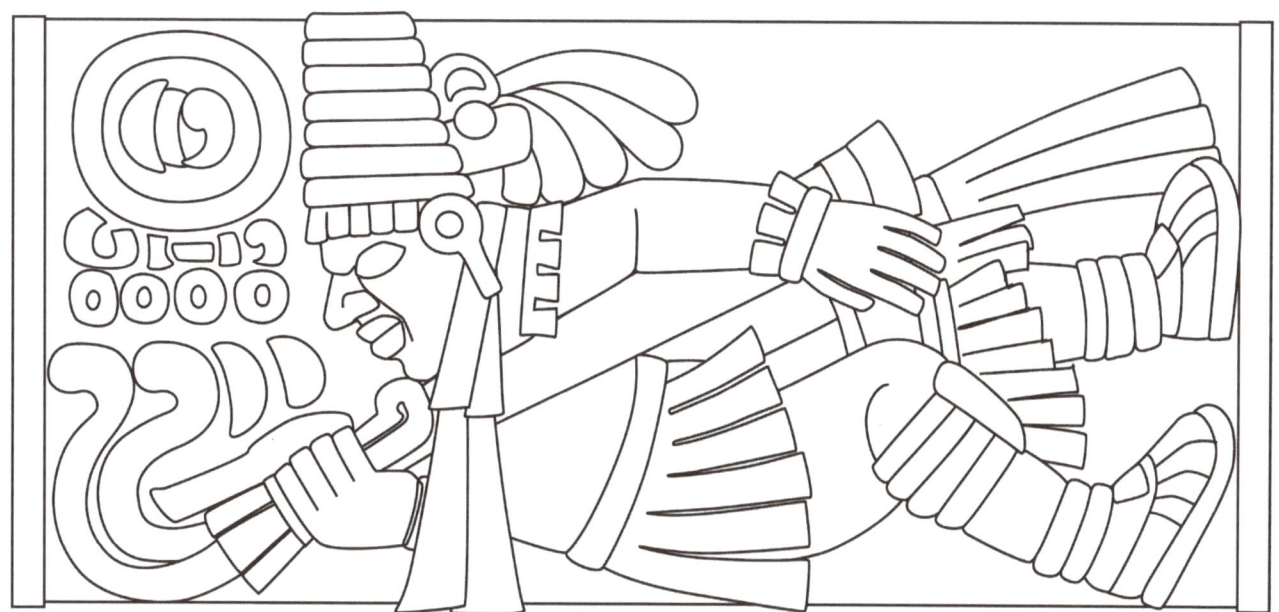

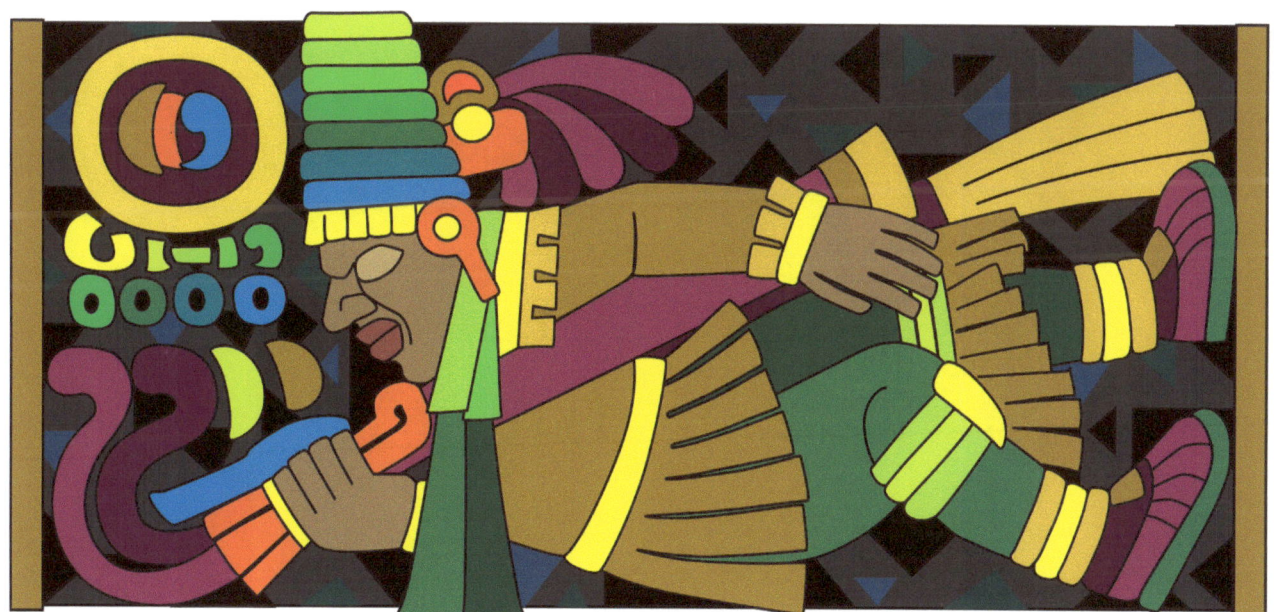

Toltec warrior, Tula, Mexico.

Color the drawings above using your preferred choice of colors.

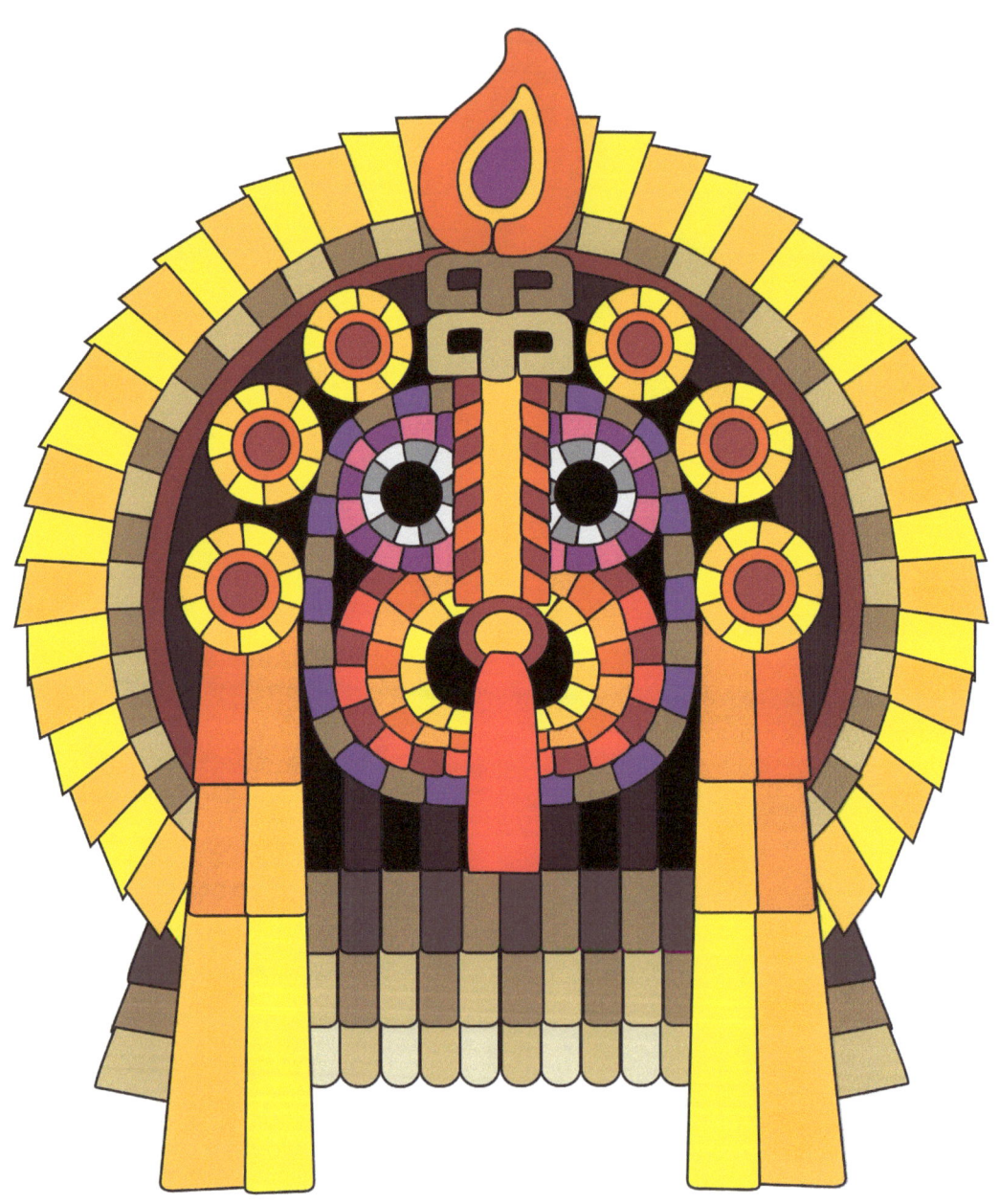

*Stylized head of a ruler as indicated by
the elaborate ornaments. Uxmal, Mexico. Between 800 - 900 C.E.*

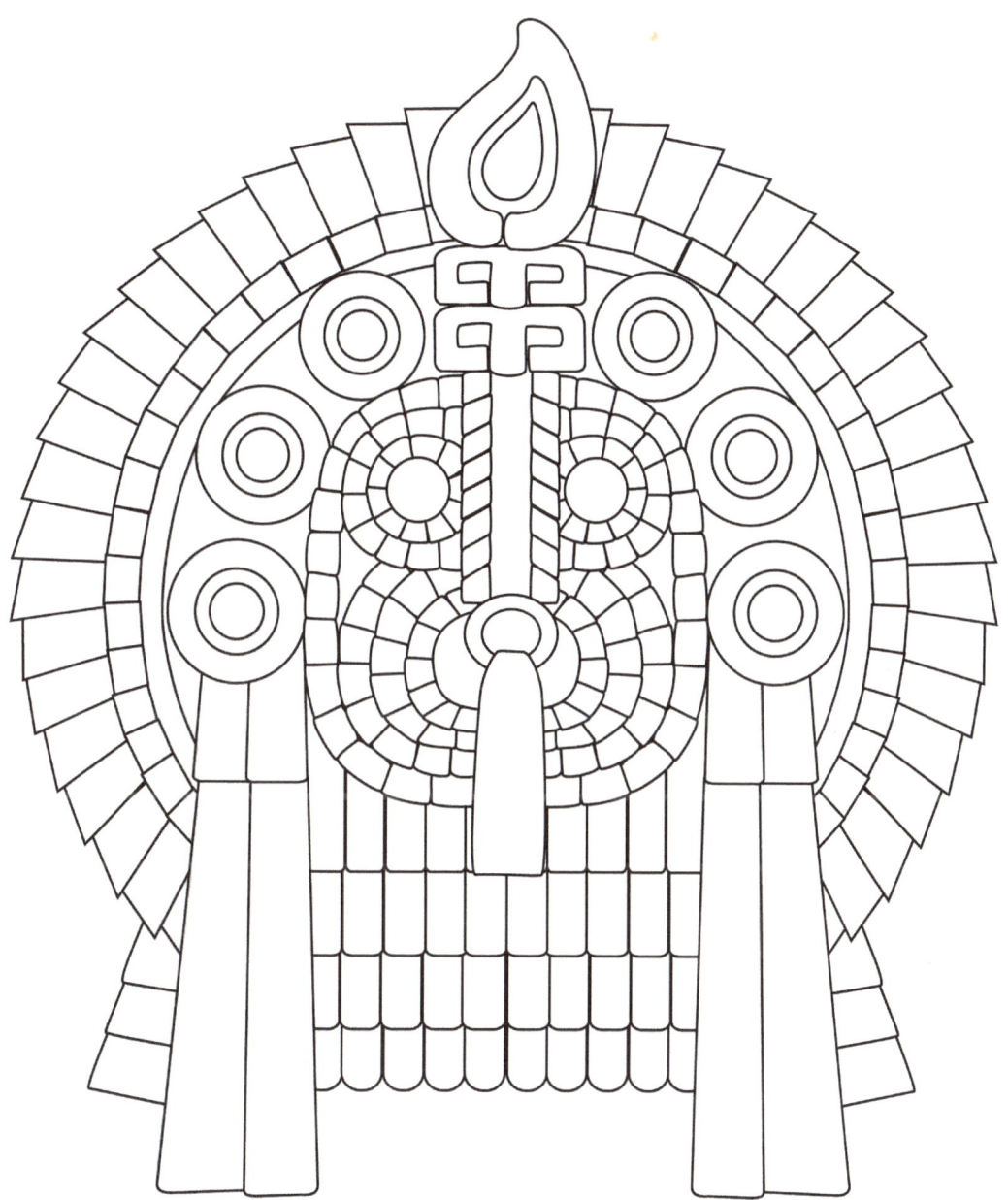

Color the drawing above using your preferred choice of colors.

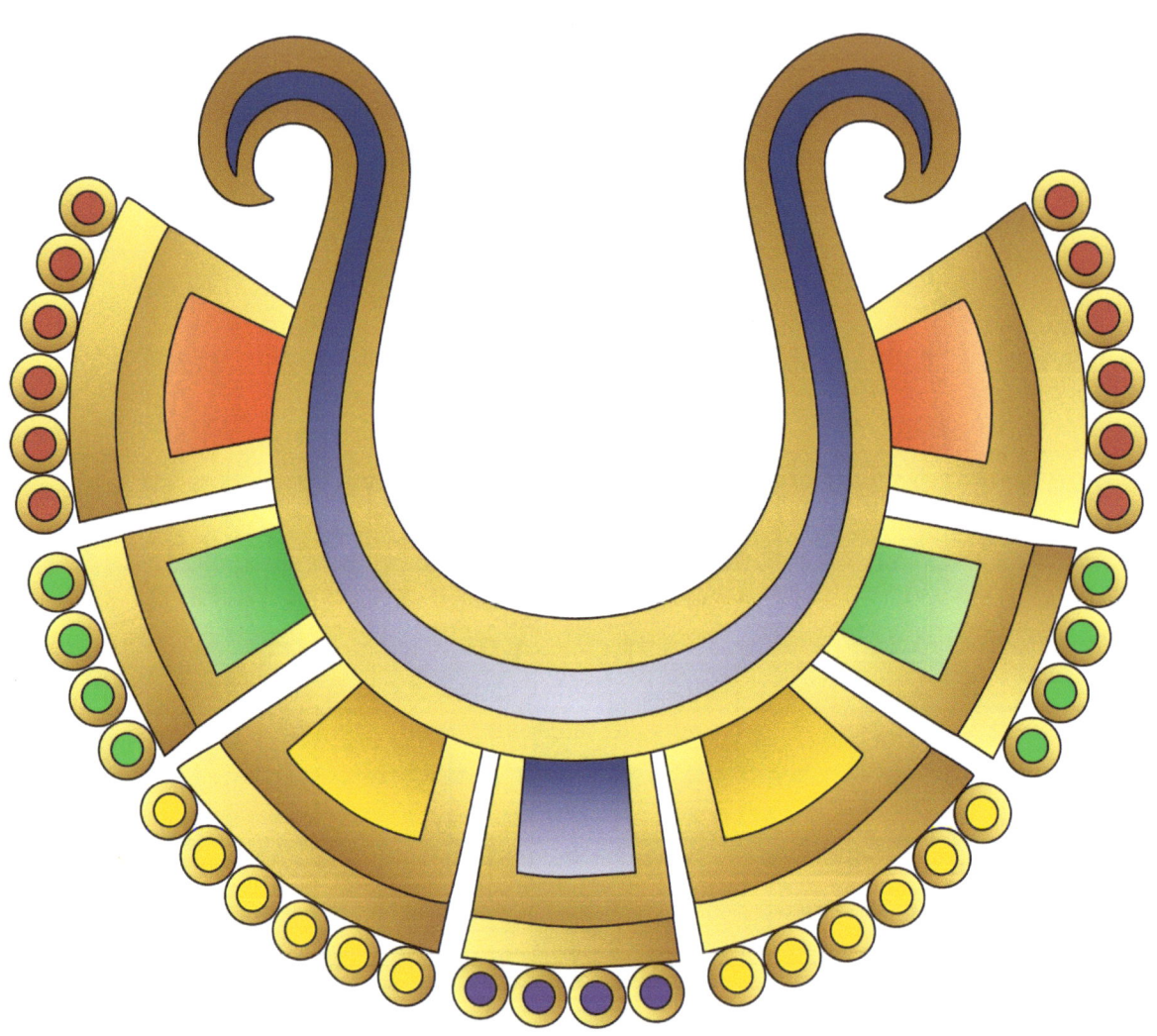

In the moneyless society of the Aztecs, gold and silver symbolized wealth. This is an Aztec necklace.

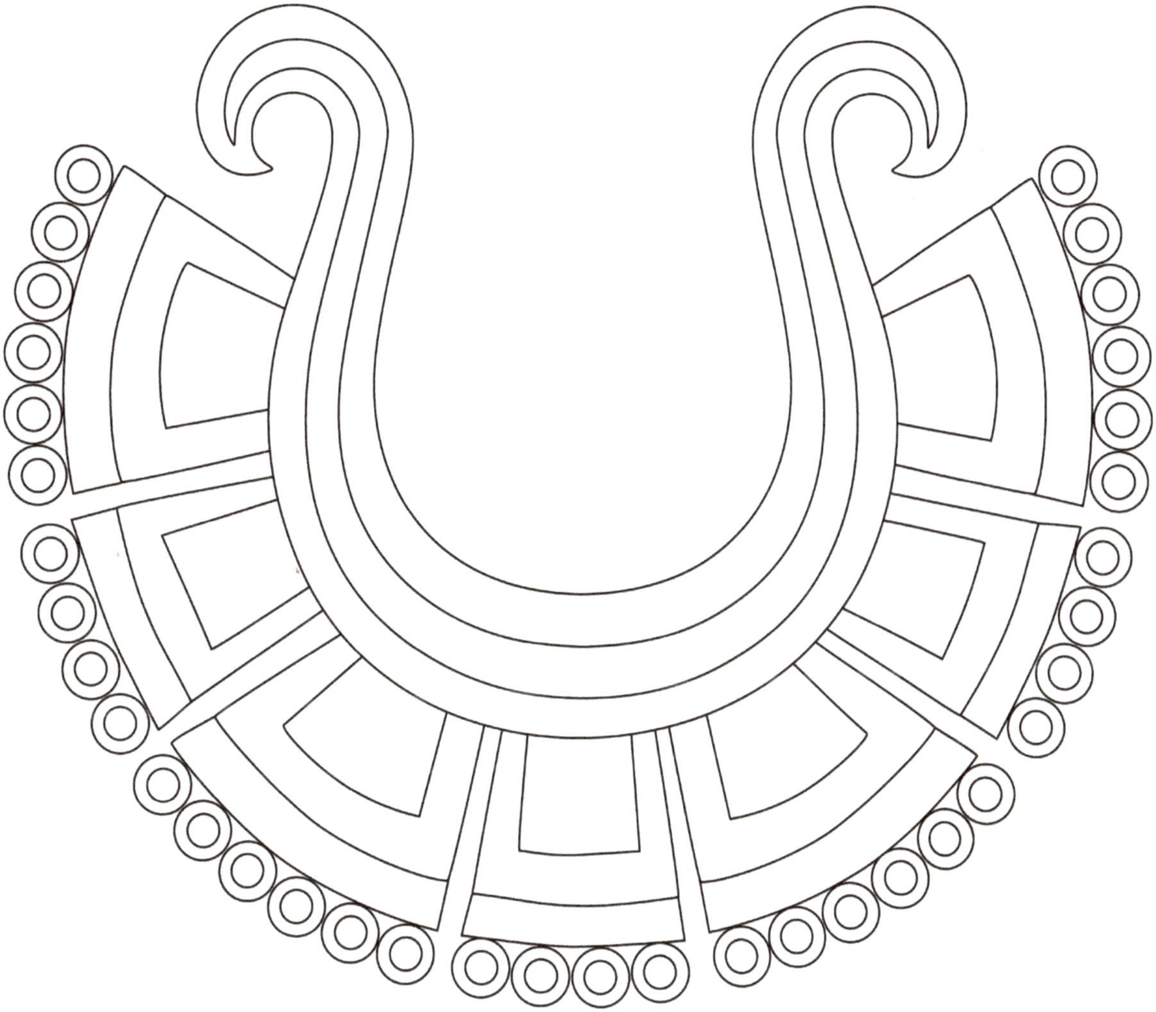

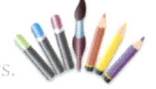

Color the drawing above using your preferred choice of colors.

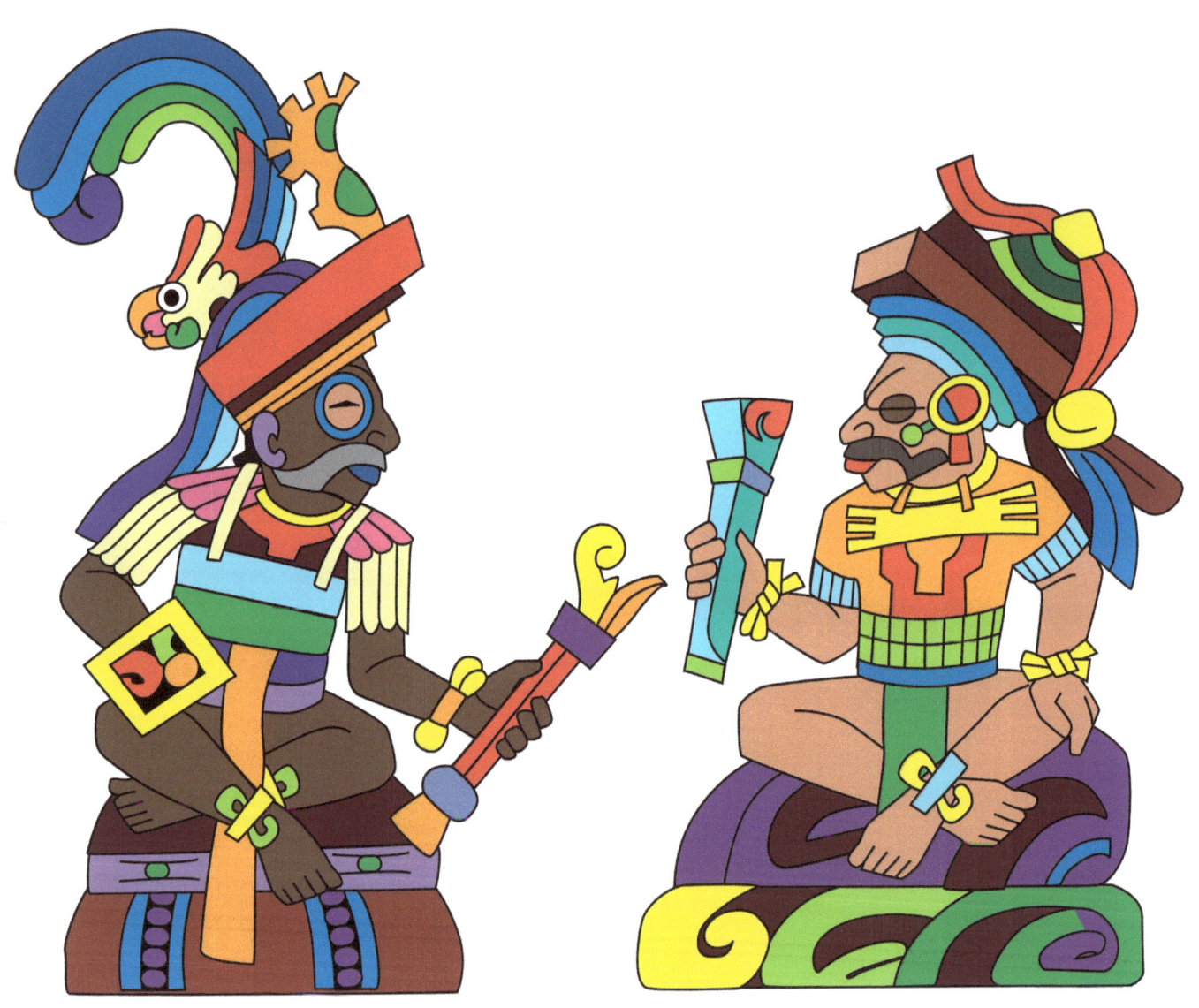

Relief on srone representing Copan Dynasty rulers. Middle of 7th Century C.E.
Dates and names of the rulers have been idenlifyed deciphering the hieroglyphics.

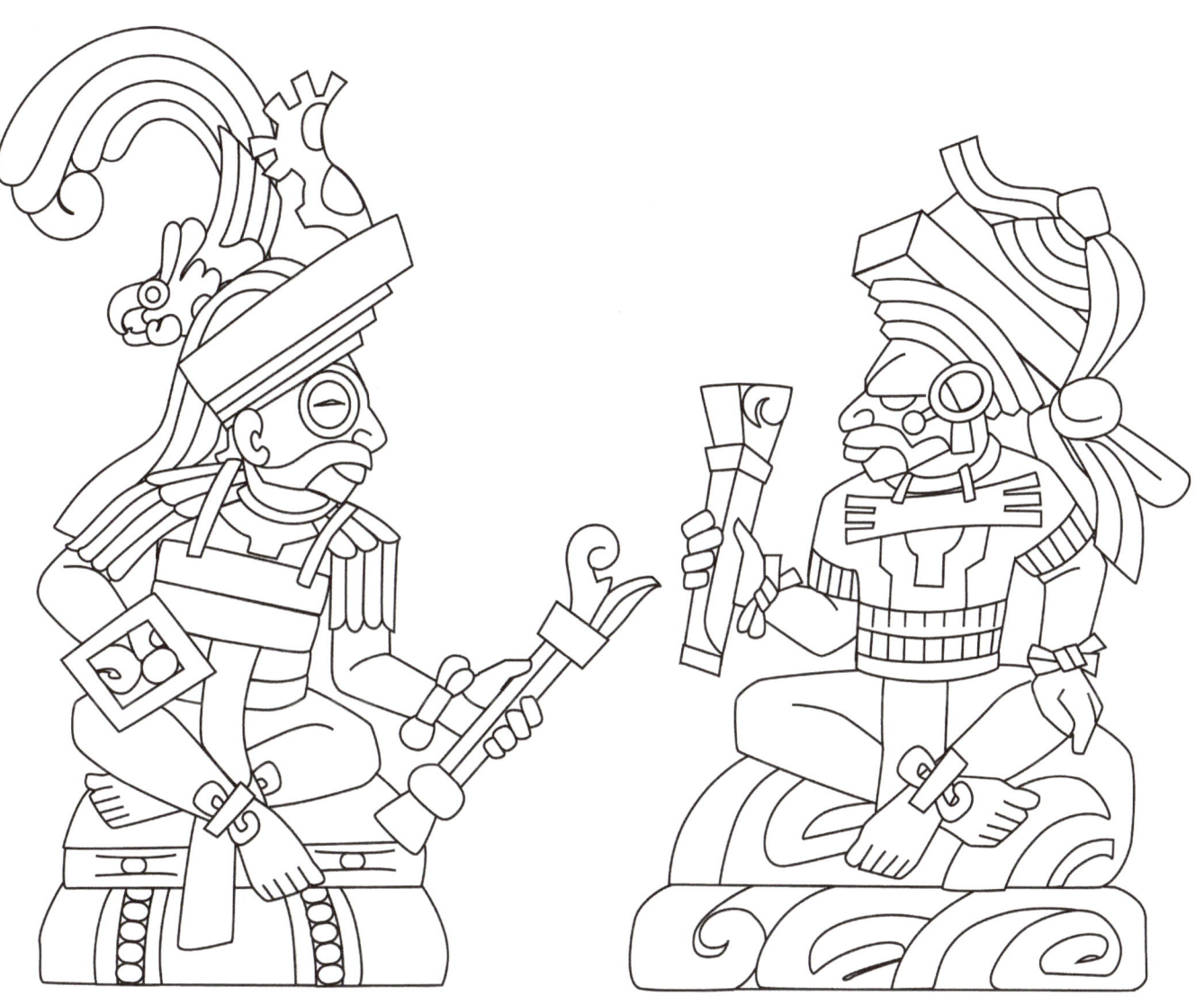

Color the drawings above using your preferred choice of colors.

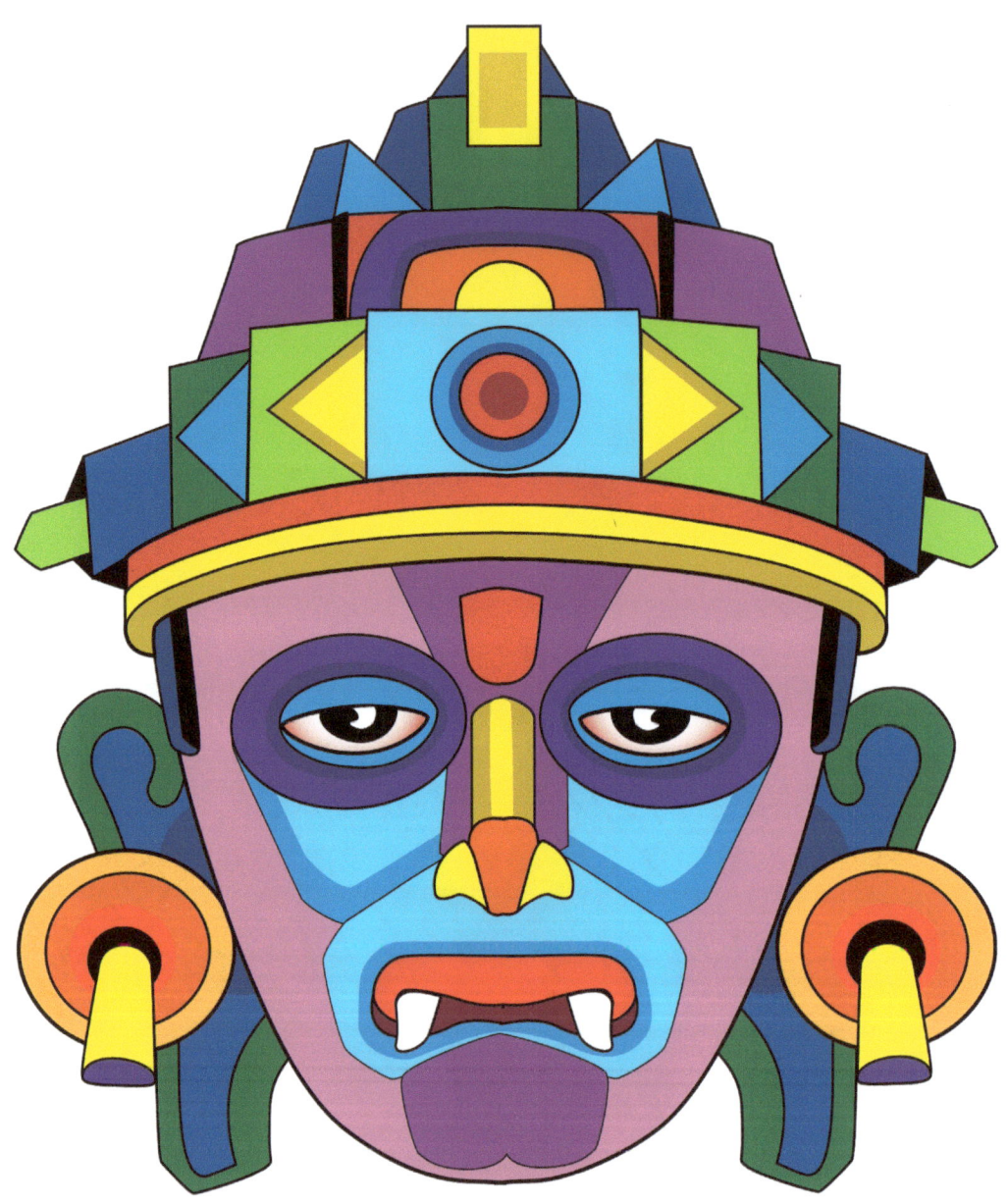

Tlaloc, the Rain God. Artists have given him a gentle spring shower as well as the devastating storm. Found at Mayapan.

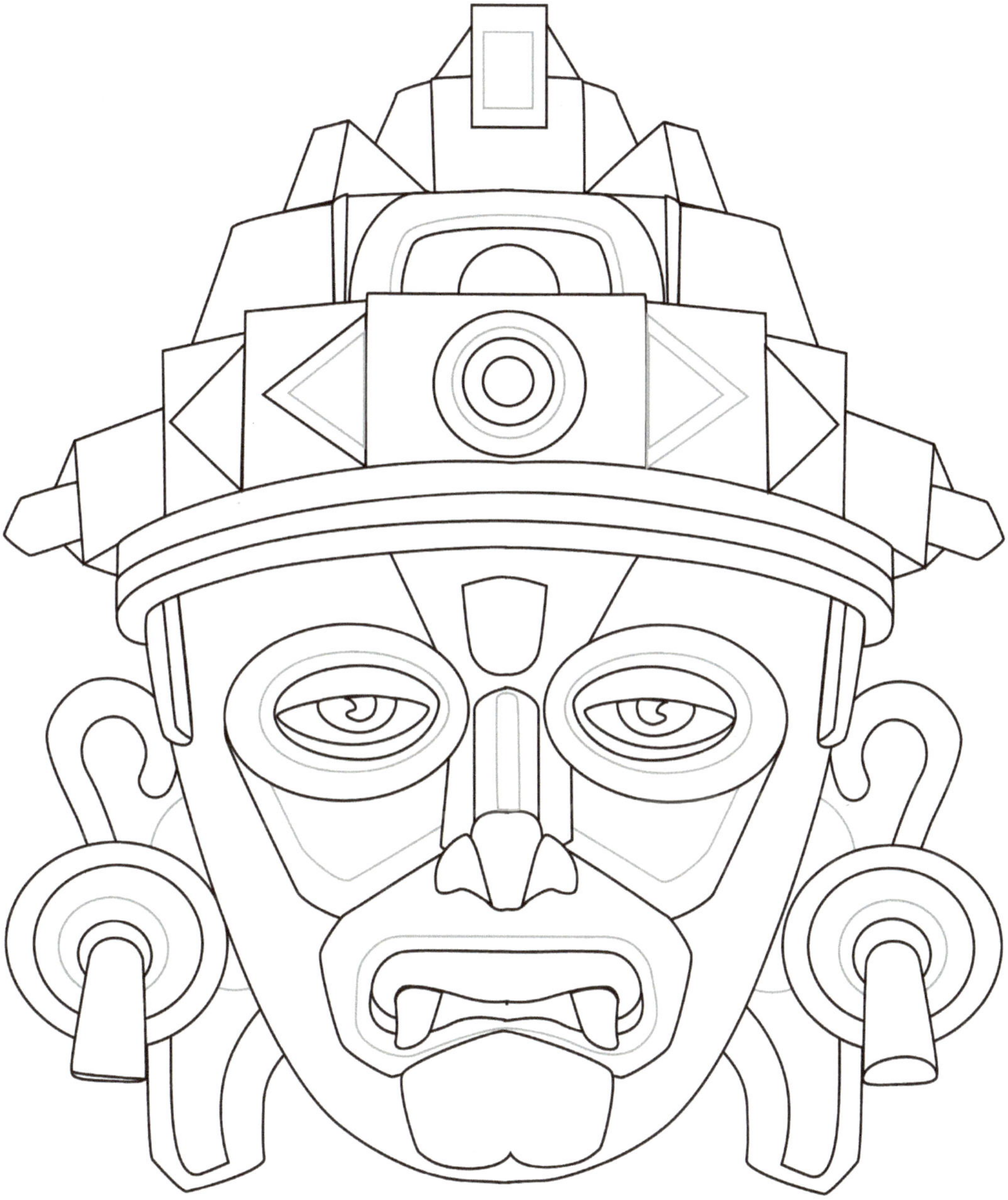

Color the drawing above using your preferred choice of colors.

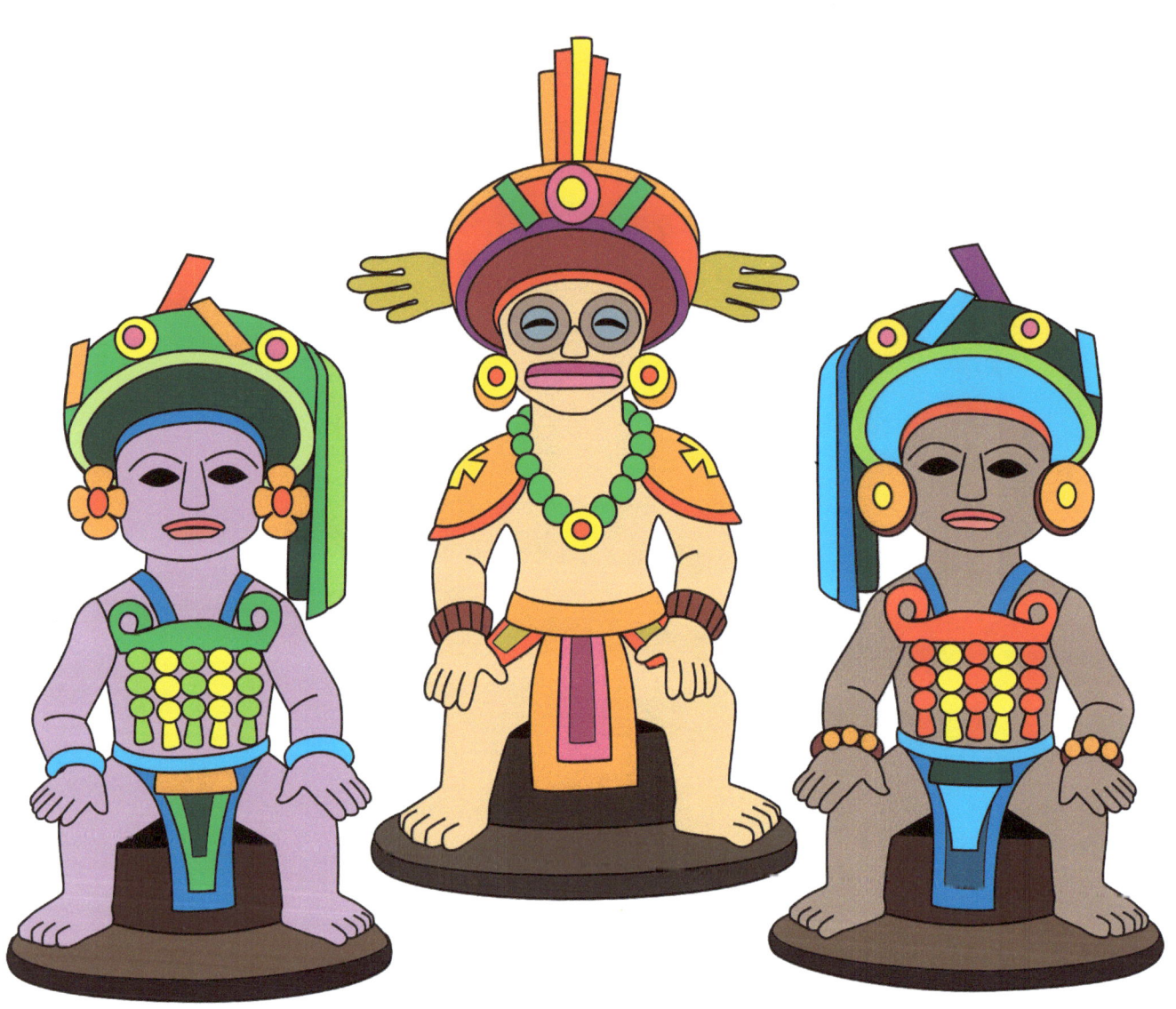

Terracotta figurines found in the city of Copan, ancient Mayan Civilization, Mexico. Possibly figurines are of the Copan rulers.

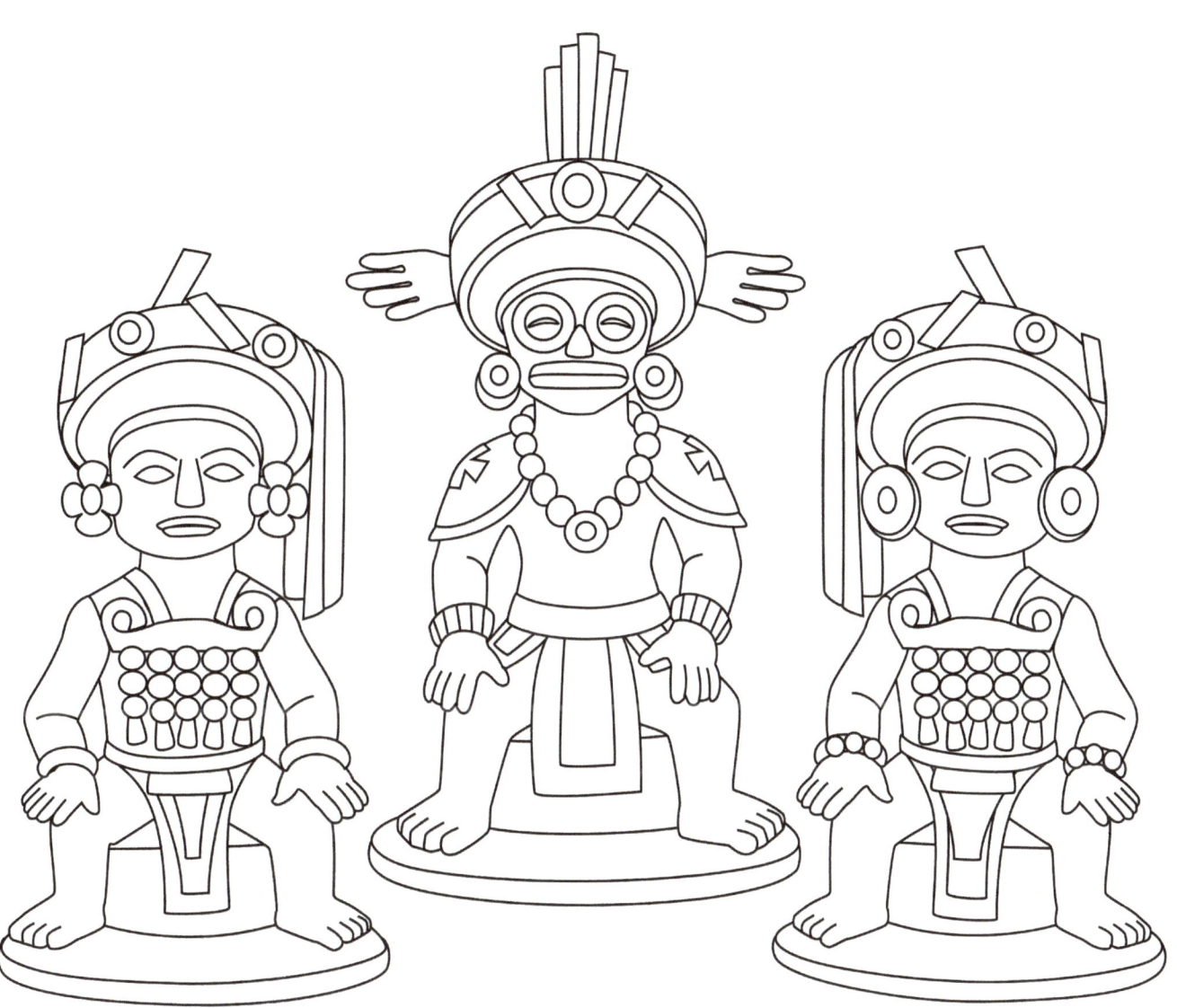

Color the drawings above using your preferred choice of colors.

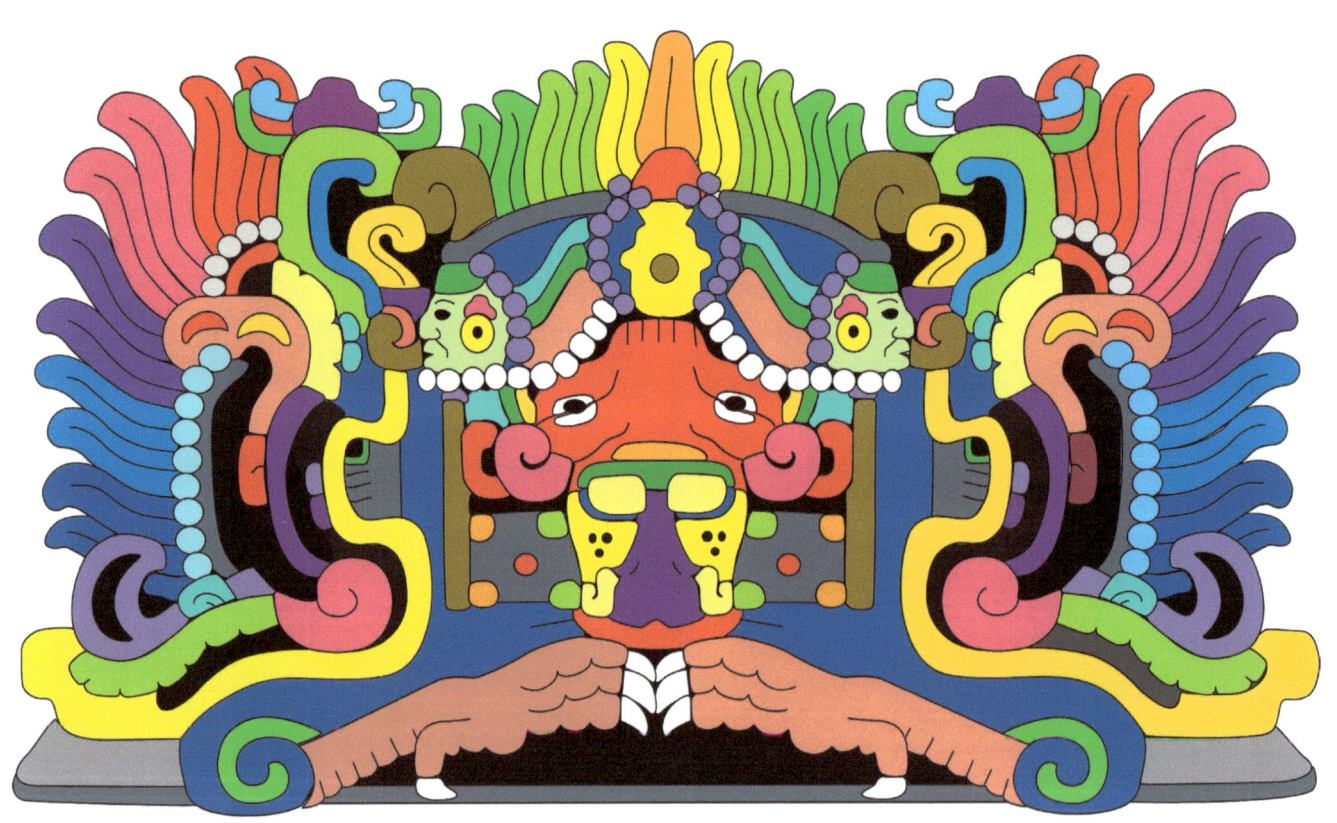

Mayan Stela. Such ornate designs are characteristic of early Mayan art from 300 - 600 C.E.

Pre-Columbian Art

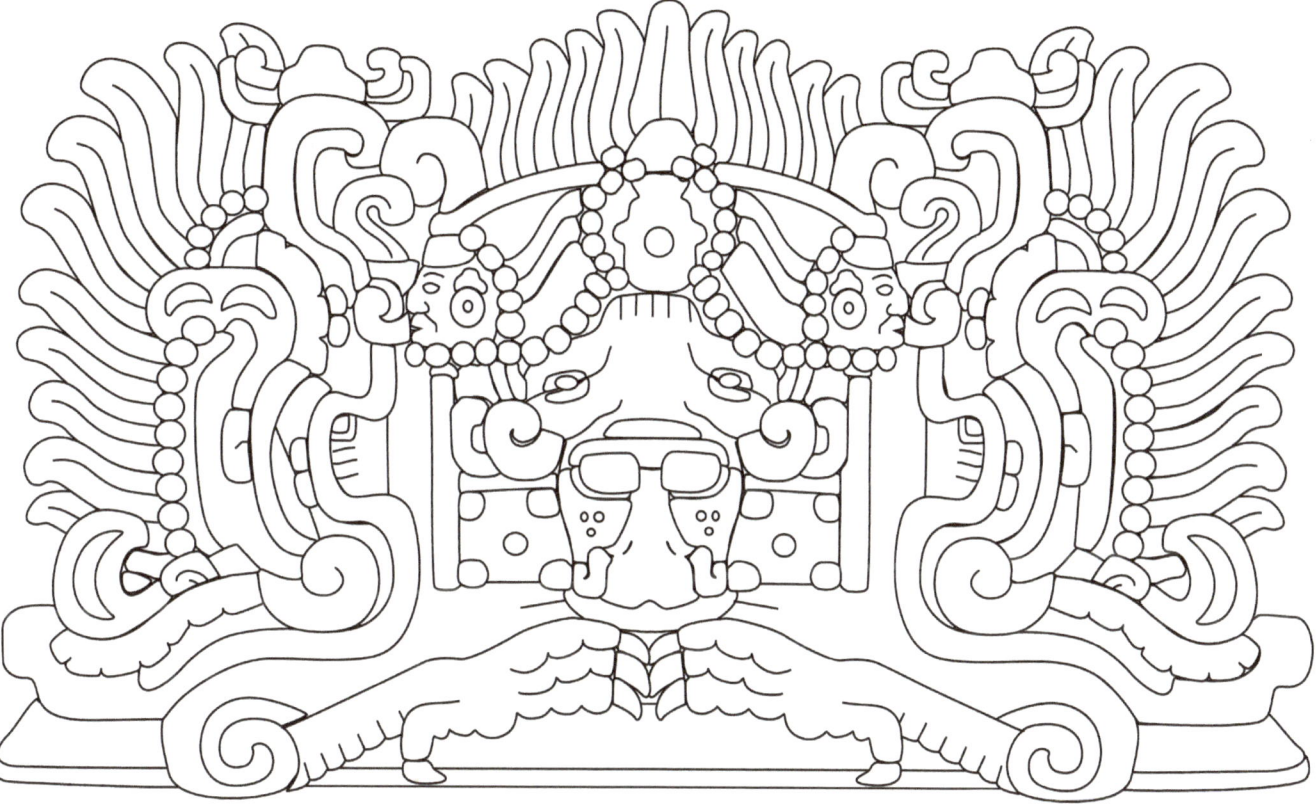

Color the drawing above using your preferred choice of colors.

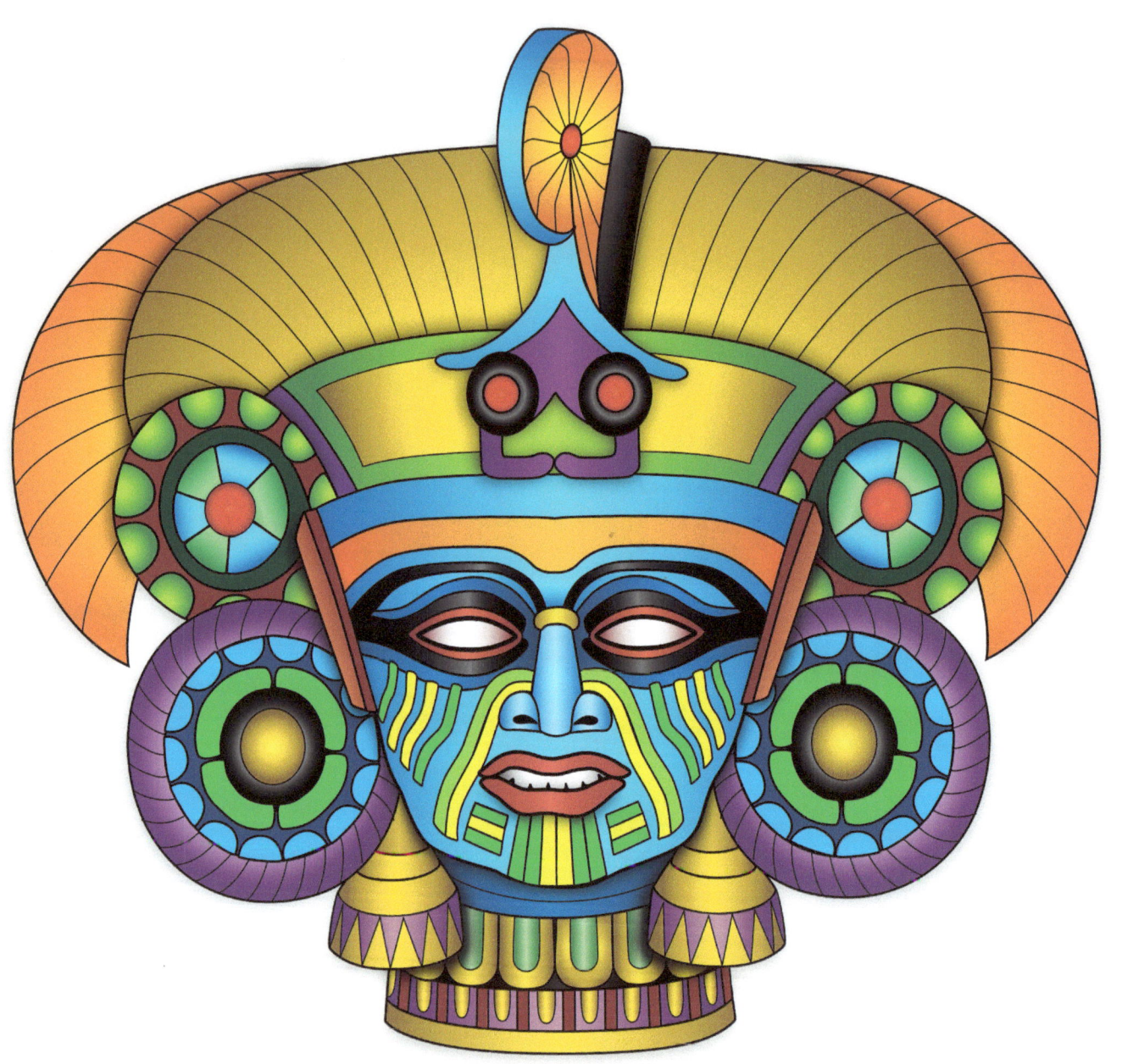

Quetzalpapalotl, the Quetzal-butterfly Aztec god, decorated top and bottom with tributes of the deity. The plume protruding from the headdress is a stylized butterfly proboscis.

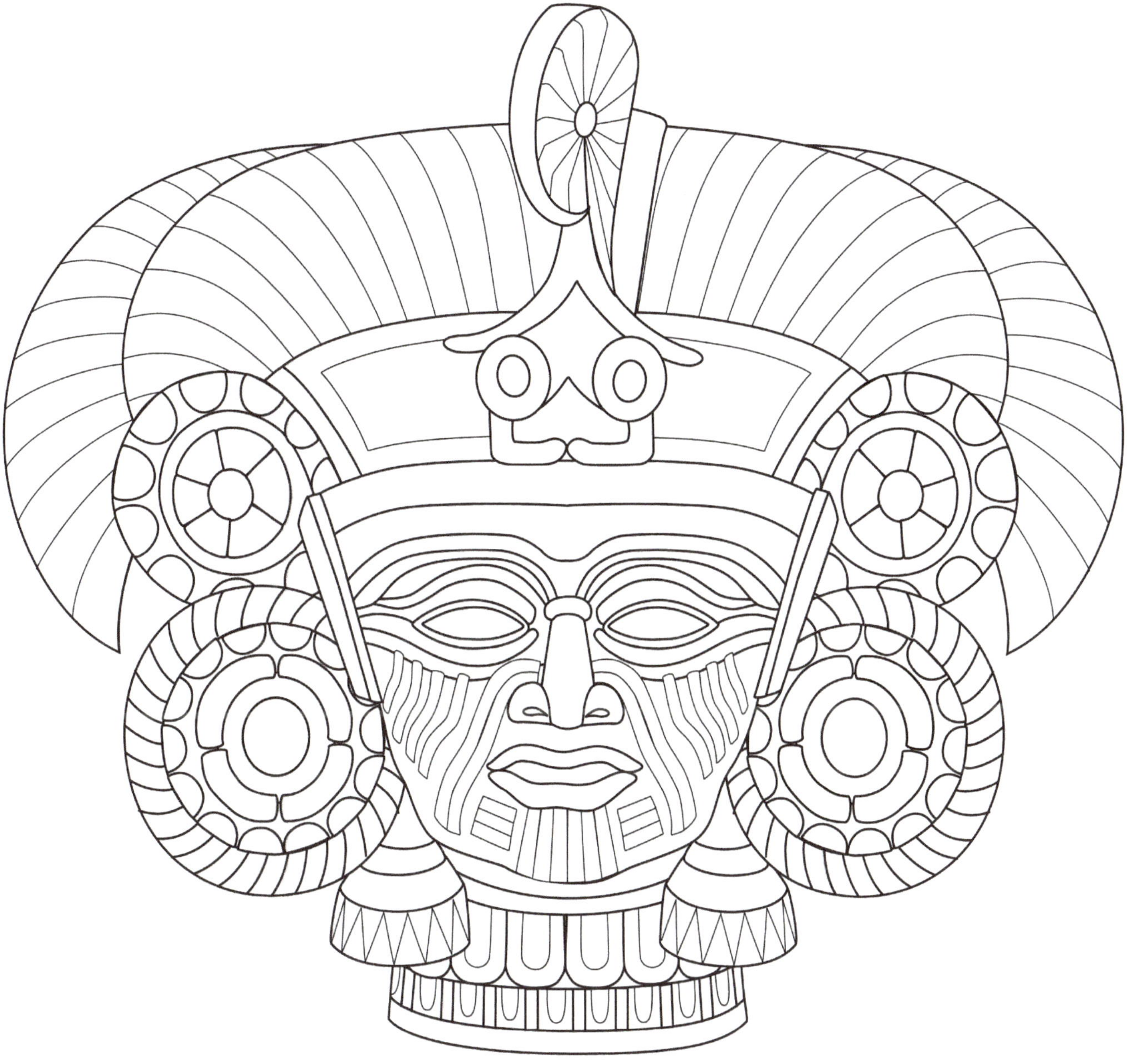

Color the drawing above using your preferred choice of colors.

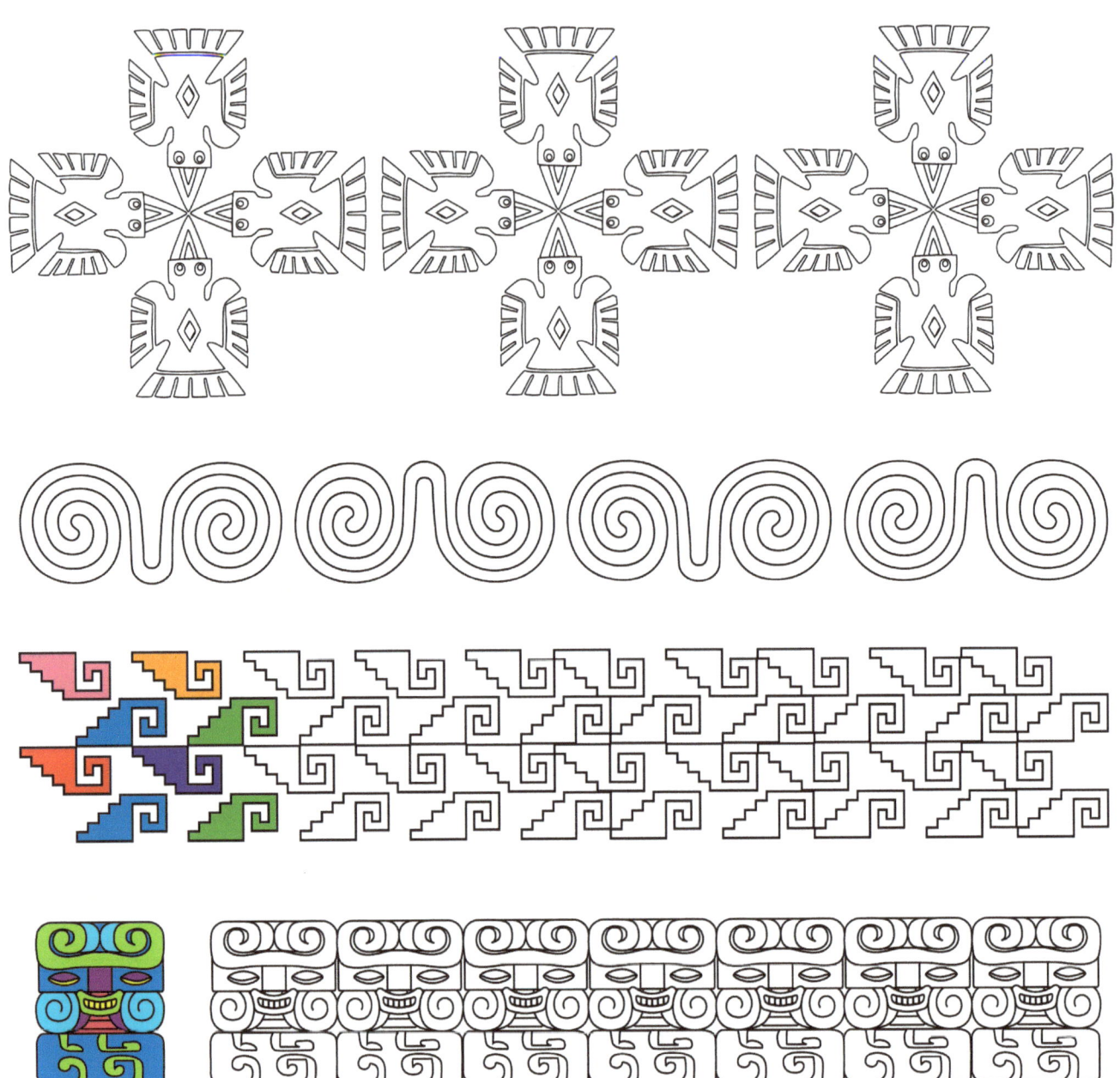

Using these images as examples, create your own piece using the elements found in Pre-Columbian Art.

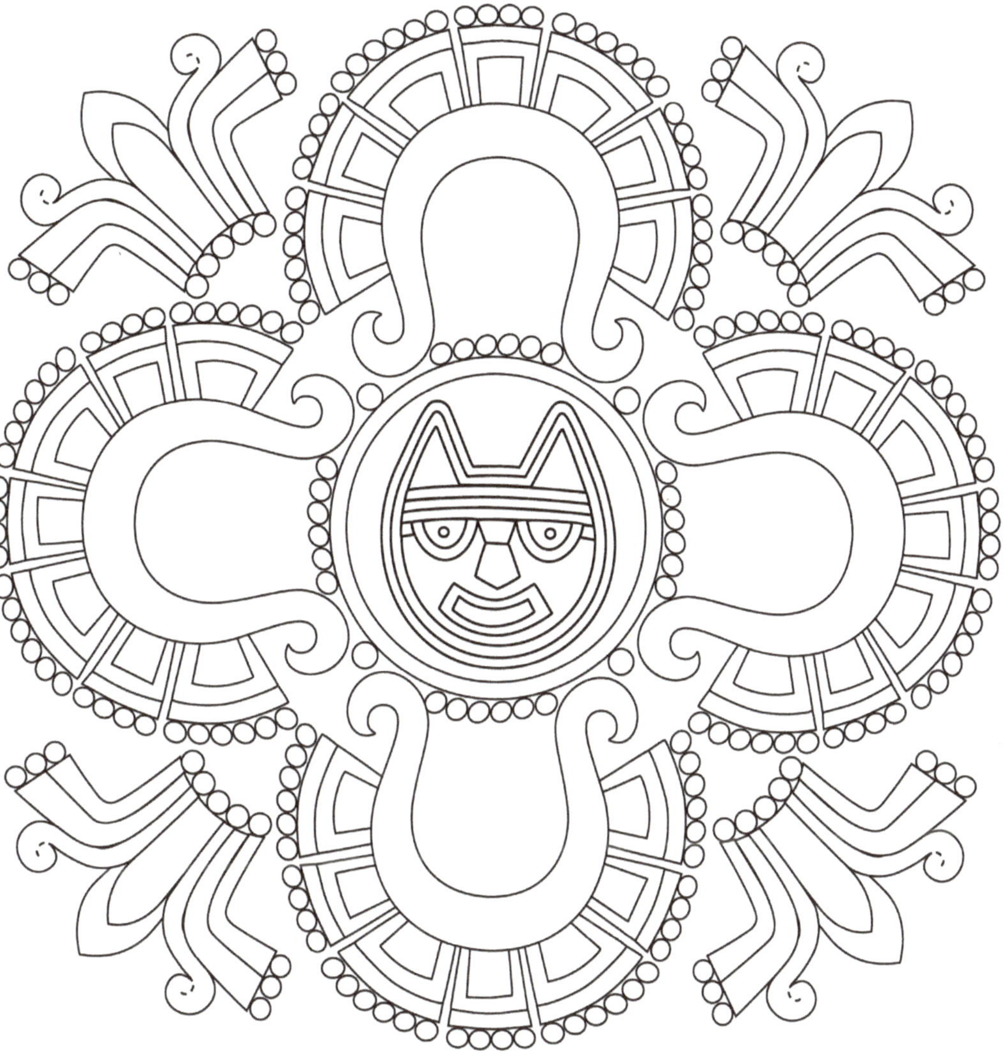

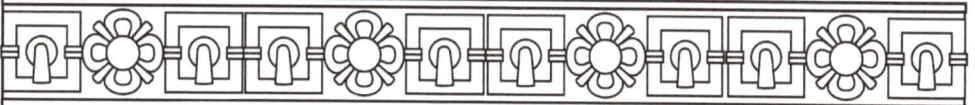

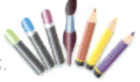
Color the drawings above using your preferred choice of colors.

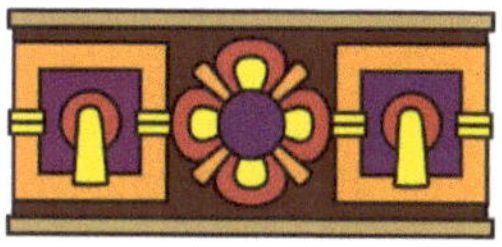

= a synopsis of =
Pre-Columbian Art

The Pre-Columbian Civilization evolved in America in total isolation. It began in 2500 B.C.E., and survived till 1500 C.E., and includes Mayan, Aztec, and Inca Civilizations.

Mayan art is considered to be one of the most beautiful and sophisticated arts of the ancient Western hemisphere. Mayan Civilization began to flourish in Peten around 1000 B.C.E. It experienced the most development from 200 B.C.E. to 700 C.E., as early classic period, and from 700 C.E. till 10th Century C.E., as the late classic period. Mayan relics can be found scattered throughout Mexico, Guatemala, Honduras, Belize and El Salvador.

During this period, Mayan pottery, sculpture, and writings bloomed as well. Mayans achieved in the arts and their science surpassed all other Pre-Columbian cultures. Mayan writings have been preserved on stone stelae, molded stucco relief embellishments, wooden doors, ceramic vessels and jade ornaments. Mayan hieroglyphic writing comprised of 800 - 1000 symbols, out of which about 200 have been deciphered.

Pre-Columbian Mesoamerican calendar was composed of eighteen months. Each day had a name and they were represented by a unique symbol. Mayan sculptures were masterpieces that were carved out of different materials like, stone, wood, and jade. Mayan paintings inside the caves and temples depicted scenes of mythology, battles, and sacrifice through vivid colors. The Olmecs, founders of Mesoamerica's first civilization were also Mexico's first sculptors. Using simple tools, they carved volcanic basalt into huge monuments, including colossal portrait heads and alters, and turned the stone into highly polished work of art.

Aztec people were composed of seven tribes. The predatory Aztec tribe left the legendary city of Chicomoztoc and settled on an island in Lake Texcoco, a site in modern Mexico city. Tenochtitlan was the capital of the Aztecs, and was founded in 1325 C.E. The most intricately carved Aztec relic is the circular stone called, The Calendar Stone. The glyphs and the icons adorned it were a road map of the Aztecs destiny. It was discovered in 1790 C.E., beneath Mexico City's central square. Aztec pyramids were known as houses of the Gods and the twin temples dedicated to two gods.

Like the Aztecs, the Incas developed the last empire in Peru at about 1000 C.E. The Incas were the natives of the region extending from Lake Titicaca to Huaraz, settled in the Curico valley where they found their capital. The Inca states extended their empire from Ecuador in the North all the way to Chile in the South.

OTHER TITLES IN THIS SERIES

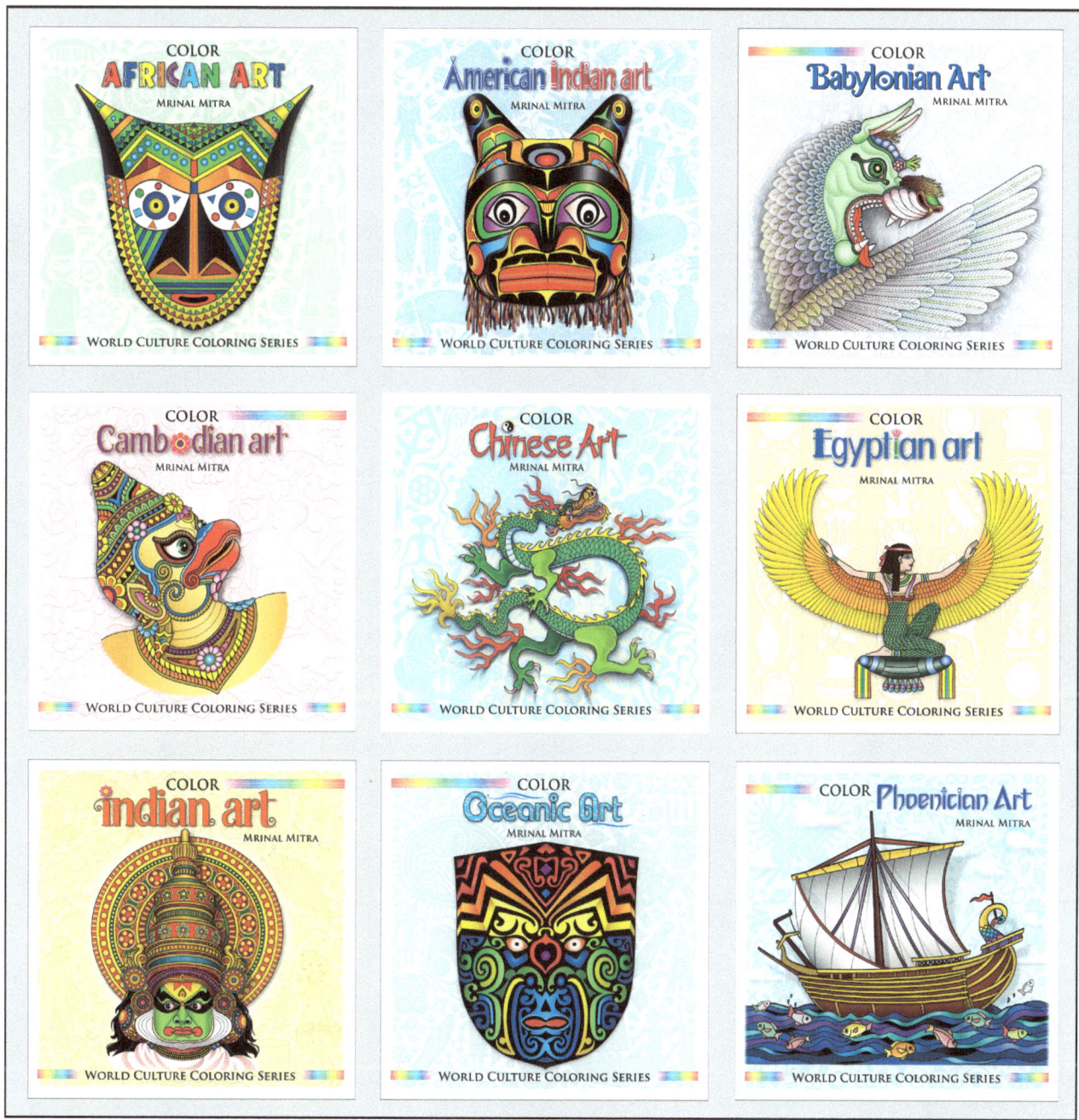

COLOR
AFRICAN ART
MRINAL MITRA
WORLD CULTURE COLORING SERIES

COLOR
American Indian art
MRINAL MITRA
WORLD CULTURE COLORING SERIES

COLOR
Babylonian Art
MRINAL MITRA
WORLD CULTURE COLORING SERIES

COLOR
Cambodian art
MRINAL MITRA
WORLD CULTURE COLORING SERIES

COLOR
Chinese Art
MRINAL MITRA
WORLD CULTURE COLORING SERIES

COLOR
Egyptian art
MRINAL MITRA
WORLD CULTURE COLORING SERIES

COLOR
Indian art
MRINAL MITRA
WORLD CULTURE COLORING SERIES

COLOR
Oceanic Art
MRINAL MITRA
WORLD CULTURE COLORING SERIES

COLOR **Phoenician Art**
MRINAL MITRA
WORLD CULTURE COLORING SERIES

AVAILABLE FROM AMAZON.COM, CREATESPACE.COM, AND OTHER RETAIL OUTLETS

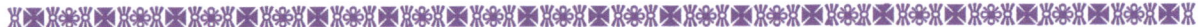

Acknowledgement

First and foremost, this series would not be possible without the number of great historical art found within the different cultural regions around the world.

In addition, we would like to acknowledge the variety of publishing's from all over the world for allowing us to learn about their fascinating ancestral art and culture. With this provided knowledge, we have hoped to have represented the art as splendidly as you have supplied it.

About the Author

Mrinal Mitra has earned a number of prestigious awards, both Indian and International, and received honors for his outstanding illustrations. Some of his recognitions include; The Noma Concours Award, Japan (twice), Illustrators Award, and Children's Choice Award, India, and honors from German Television "Transtel", BRNO- CSSR, TIBI- Iran, and UNICEF, New York.

Many of his talented artworks have been exhibited in several different countries such as; India, Japan, Italy, Czech Republic, Iran, and New Zealand. Mitra has authored, designed and illustrated trade and educational children's books for many Indian as well as Multinational Book Publishers around the globe.

Copyright: Mrinal Mitra, 2014

Printed by CreateSpace, An Amazon.com. Company
Available from Amazon.com, CreateSpace.com, and other retail outlets

For further inquiry please contact Mrinal Mitra at: mitra_mrinal@hotmail.com

www.ingramcontent.com/pod-product-compliance
Lightning Source LLC
Chambersburg PA
CBHW050840180526
45159CB00004B/1973